Mutiny in the Mountains

West Virginia Public Workers, 1969–2019

Gordon Simmons

Mutiny in the Mountains: West Virginia Public Workers, 1969–2019

ISBN: 979-8-88744-153-5 (paperback)
ISBN: 979-8-88744-154-2 (ebook)
Library of Congress Control Number: 2025936234

Cover design by John Yates / stealworks.com
Interior design by briandesign

10 9 8 7 6 5 4 3 2 1

PM Press
PO Box 23912
Oakland, CA 94623
www.pmpress.org

Printed in the USA.

To Karen Kelly

Contents

Acknowledgments

The phrase appropriated for the initial working title for this book, "a rebellion against government," was lifted from the *Kirker* decision regarding the 1969 state road walkout wherein it was quoted from an earlier ruling as a general appraisal of public worker strikes. It was virtually identical to Federal Reserve chair Arthur Burns's description of the 1970 national postal worker wildcat strike as "an insurrection against Government."

It would require a separate monograph to adequately acknowledge the depth and range of scholarship on West Virginia labor history upon which the present study depends, but I will limit myself to acknowledging two historians whose works have been indispensable to my education. The late Fred Barkey was both my first instructor in West Virginia labor history and—in the years that followed—a valued friend and comrade. Dave Corbin was a close second to Fred in both influence and friendship until his recent passing. Neither of these should be held responsible for any of my assertions, opinions, or conclusions.

The number of fellow workers, scholars, writers, librarians, activists and friends, who contributed to my practical and intellectual formation is far too great to allow an adequate listing of those to whom I am indebted.

This project is being presented with financial assistance from the West Virginia Humanities Council, a state affiliate of the National Endowment for the Humanities. Any views, findings, conclusions or recommendations do not necessarily represent those of the West Virginia Humanities Council or the National Endowment for the Humanities.

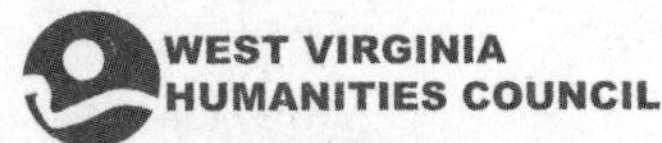

List of Abbreviations

AFL-CIO	American Federation of Labor–Congress of Industrial Organizations
AFGE	American Federation of Government Employees
AFSCME	American Federation of State, County and Municipal Employees
AFT	American Federation of Teachers
ATU	Amalgamated Transit Union
CWA	Communications Workers of America
DHHR	West Virginia Department of Health and Human Resources
DOH	West Virginia Division of Highways
IWW	Industrial Workers of the World
NEA	National Education Association
NCPSWU	North Carolina Public Service Workers Union
NLRB	National Labor Relations Board
NUHHCE	National Union of Hospital and Health Care Employees
PEIA	Public Employees Insurance Agency
RWDSU	Retail, Wholesale and Department Store Union
SEIU	Service Employees International Union
SPB	West Virginia State Personnel Board
TWAP	Transportation Worker Apprenticeship Program
UE	United Electrical, Radio and Machine Workers of America
UMWA	United Mine Workers of America
UPWA	United Public Workers of America
USU	United Staff Union

WVEA	West Virginia Education Association
WVPEA	West Virginia Public Employees Association
WVPWU	West Virginia Public Workers Union
WVSEU	West Virginia State Employees Union
WVSSPA	West Virginia School Service Personnel Association
WVSTA	West Virginia State Teachers Association

CHAPTER 1

A Brief Labor History of West Virginia

As Jeremy Brecher observed in the foreword to his book, *Strike!*:

> Most historians, whether radical or conservative, tend to consider ordinary workers a mere "rank and file," controlled and directed by unions and labor leaders. Strikes are presumably the work of these organizations and leaders. I have found, on the contrary, that far from fomenting strikes and rebellions, unions and labor leaders have most often striven to prevent or contain them, while the drive to extend them has generally come from a most undocile "rank and file." ... Ordinary working people, acting on their own, have through the decades thought, planned, drawn lessons from their own experiences, organized themselves, and taken action in common.... Ordinary people can have power over social life when power as we have known it—power of some people over others—is dissolved completely.[1]

A comprehensive history of class struggle in West Virginia would be beyond the scope of the present study. A concise survey of worker struggles in West Virginia that preceded the events recounted here, however, is warranted if only in order to provide some context for a more specific consideration of worker activism in West Virginia's public sector.

Marmet, West Virginia, is a town just east of the state capital of Charleston on the Kanawha River and would, in 1921, gain historical significance as the assembly point for a march of thousands striking coal miners intent on invading the antiunion stronghold of Blair Mountain, in Logan County to the south in what has been called one of the largest worker uprisings in US history. In 1876, however, that location was named Brownstown and was the site of a federal government works project constructing a lock and dam on the Kanawha and, because it was a government project, Brownstown may well have been the site of the first public worker strike in West Virginia.

According to a later newspaper account, on April 17, 1876, word spread that the contractor for the project had rebuffed demands by the workers for higher wages, which had led to a strike by hundreds of men employed on the project. The out-of-state contractor, D.M. Dull, had first sought to break the strike by importing Black workers from Virginia, but that effort reportedly lasted only a day as strikers took control of the property and the strikebreakers fled. The contractor then appealed to the county sheriff who deputized nearly a hundred armed men, commandeered a steamboat, and proceeded to invade the strike zone. The sheriff's armed force arrested four strikers deemed to be leaders and ordered the remainder of the strikers back to work. Although the arrested strikers were released without trial, they brought their own charges of false imprisonment against Dull. The following year, on November 14, 1877, after those cases were moved to federal court because the events had occurred on government property, the first case of the strikers, that of Philip O'Riley, was decided. He was denied his claim by a jury that had been instructed by the judge on what verdict to deliver, and O'Riley was fined by the court for legal costs. The charges brought by the rest were dismissed without the benefit of trial.[2]

Martinsburg Rail Strike

Visitors to the site of the historic Martinsburg train station of the Baltimore and Ohio Railroad might chance upon an official state historical marker commemorating a July 17, 1877, work stoppage, the beginning of what arguably became the nation's first general strike and is sometimes referred to by historians as the Great Upheaval. The side of the marker commemorating the strike is, unfortunately, accessible only by leaning out precariously over the railing of an elevated platform, a fact which, on consideration, is symptomatic of a long tradition of obscurity regarding the actual history of the state's working people in their struggle against economic and political domination by corporations.

The 1870s had been, to be sure, a period of extended economic depression. Despite that, the railroad corporations were doing comparatively well at the time, with major players like the B&O paying steady dividends to their stockholders throughout the economic downturn. Those same corporations were also cutting wages of their workers repeatedly throughout the period from 1873 to 1877, and the reductions reached double-digit percentages.[3]

The Martinsburg strike began when rail workers learned of an additional 10 percent pay cut, the second such wage reduction by the B&O in less than a year. On news of this wage reduction, the workers suddenly refused to operate the trains, uncoupled their engines, placed the yard under occupation and effectively halted train traffic on the line, all in defiance of the arrival of the mayor with local police in tow. The next day, the strike continued, and the railway shutdown was by then enforced by hundreds of rail workers and sympathetic townspeople publicly gathering for that purpose.[4]

After state militia were called and dispatched, there were shots exchanged between the soldiers and strikers, with one striker killed, but the line remained closed and the militia withdrew. The Martinsburg rail blockade held, and, as word spread quickly, there were shutdowns all along the B&O line, particularly in Wheeling, where even nonrailroad workers were already on strike, and as a result, a general strike of all workers spread.

The railroad called for federal troops to intervene, given the abject failure of the state militia—which was mostly composed of working people called up on temporary notice and therefore found to be unreliable for purposes of strikebreaking—to end the work stoppage. Nevertheless, the strike by rail workers and others continued to spread, to Pennsylvania, Maryland, New York, and west to St. Louis, where the entire city fell under the control of the striking workers. One of the activists who joined the general strike as it spread to Chicago was Albert Parsons, companion of Lucy Parsons, and one those who would later be executed in the wake of an 1886 Haymarket demonstration on behalf of the eight-hour workday.[5] The strike even provoked work stoppages as far away as Iowa and Canada. One of the most remarkable features of what began in Martinsburg, West Virginia, was the speed by which the strike spread in addition to the magnitude of the events it provoked elsewhere.[6]

Coming six years after the Paris Commune, the 1877 general strike raised alarm among capitalists and their agencies of government and the press. It also found a voice in workers' proclamations issued during the course of events: "It was a grand sight to see in West Virginia, white and colored men standing together, men of all nationalities in one supreme contest for the common rights of workingmen."[7]

The intervention of federal troops mobilized by President Harding finally suppressed the strike a month and a half after its outbreak. It would not, however, be the last time that a strike unsanctioned by either law or union officials that started in West Virginia would reverberate across America. The 1877 general strike was in that respect an instance of worker-initiated work stoppage that would come to be called, especially after the later New Deal regime of labor relations codified in the National Labor Relations Act of 1935, a "wildcat strike."

In recounting the origin and spread of the 1877 strike, Brecher draws attention to what ought to be obvious but is nevertheless often overlooked. The strike was the spontaneous and self-directed collective activity of the workers themselves. No one gave orders; no political party bosses or union leaders issued instructions mobilizing the workers. It was, in other words, an unpredicted—and given the apparent previous acquiescence by workers to continually worsening conditions and pay in the preceding period—an unanticipated "upheaval" spontaneously erupting without leaders.[8] It was an instance of what Jean-Paul Sartre would later describe as a "group-in-fusion."[9] The strike was also one of the earliest and most dramatic examples of the exercise of workers power in

American history. Up to that point, as Daniel Guerin has pointed out, railroad workers had little formal union organization apart from craft-defined "brotherhoods." In the wake of the general strike, there was an attempt to create an industry-wide union. But as importantly, the 1877 general strike "heralded an unprecedented unity between skilled and unskilled workers as the factory proletariat, still unorganized, fought side by side with the trainmen."[10]

It was apt that the first major episode in West Virginia labor history involved railway workers, given that so much of the subsequent industrialization of the state was facilitated and enabled by the growth of rail transportation. It might be an exaggeration to regard, after the 1877 general strike, West Virginia's next century of class struggle as predominantly the story of coal miners, but it would also be only a slight exaggeration. The state's industrial history endured episodes of salt, oil and gas, and timber extraction, and railroad and river transportation development, as well as glass and steel manufacturing, all of which were accompanied by labor issues that ran the gamut from chattel slavery to wage labor, but nothing imposed the political and economic dominance of market forces in central Appalachia quite so thoroughly and definitively as the coal industry.[11]

Paint Creek and Cabin Creek

The internal development of railroads in West Virginia that began in the late nineteenth century eventually provided the necessary means for the integration of the mountain region into capitalist markets to an extent far beyond the earlier reliance on waterway transportation as the principal means of commercial trade. Railroads also proved essential for having enabled capitalist integration to be exploitive because it was premised on the expansion of wage labor throughout Appalachian society as the most pervasive, if not the only, economic relation. It was additionally exploitive insofar as the accumulation of capital based primarily on the extraction of natural resources—first timber, then coal—became the dominant form for the realization of commercial activity in West Virginia.[12]

There are, in fact, circumstantial indications to support the thesis that Appalachia has been—by the deliberate design of economic and political elites—relegated to the status of an "internal colony," wherein interests that were engaged in extractive capital accumulation intentionally obstructed differing local industrial development, such as glass manufacturing, because, in the worst case, it could entail the introduction of radical challenges to the existing social order, or even minimally because it could introduce an upward pressure on prevailing wages in any particular region where it flourished.[13]

Coal was the fuel that industrialized and modernized America. It would be difficult to overstate the historical significance of coal mining to West Virginia socially, economically, or politically. No labor history of West Virginia, regardless of its specific focus, can ignore the context of the class struggle that occurred in coal mining. In West Virginia, two related historical developments were essential to the economic dependence occasioned by the dominance of extractive coal production. The first involved the expropriation of land and mineral rights ownership that was effected through an extensive history of legal and political conduct by capitalists and their agents. The second was the reduction of the resident population—and, over time, European immigrants and southern Black migrants—to a condition of wage labor servitude for the extraction and transport of coal.[14] Just as lawmaking and the courts had been instruments to enable and legitimize the accumulation of assets and wealth in establishing the coal industry, so too would lawmaking and the courts be vehicles to enforce the owners' dominance over what proved to be a continually restive and resistant workforce.[15]

Suffice to say that whatever the limitations of the collective organizational forms—such as the United Mine Workers of America (UMWA)—as well as the various workplace strategies that coal miners adopted to defend their interests, all were violently and repeatedly repressed in what was an unrelentingly hostile legal and political context.[16] Two episodes stand out as periods of sustained and open class warfare in West Virginia during the early twentieth century: the 1912–13 strike in Cabin and Paint creeks in Kanawha County and the extended coal mine war that swept through the southern counties of the state in 1920–21.

During the first episode, a drawn-out strike by both union and nonunion miners erupted in the coal mining communities of upper Kanawha County, triggered and sustained by the prevalent use of private mine guards employed by coal operators to quell and subdue any resistance to the feudal control exercised over the work and daily life of miners and their families, particularly those employed and residing in company-owned towns. Over the course of the uprising, the miners were forced to contend not only with the armed enforcers of the coal companies and the government. They also were faced with betrayals by the international and national offices, respectively, of the two most prominent organizations to which they had turned in order to advance their demands for more autonomy: the UMWA and the Socialist Party.[17]

Historian David Corbin's account of the 1912–13 strike places emphasis on the impact of the betrayal of the rank-and-file miners by the international office of the UMWA, which, in April, 1913, went behind their backs to work out a compromise settlement with the state's governor—who had earlier declared martial law in an effort to break the strike—and their avowed enemy, the coal operators. Sensing that the operators were about to capitulate, the strikers were understandably incensed that the compromise pact failed to address what they considered to be important demands, and so began preparations to renew the strike in rejection and defiance of the compromise settlement. Learning this, the coal operators panicked and granted all of the strikers' demands. Corbin observes that their ability to overcome the capitulation by heretofore erstwhile allies taught the West Virginians the power of solidarity that "could work, not only against the companies, but also against the state and even their own union."[18]

From Matewan to Blair Mountain

Corbin argues that workers' experiences in the 1912–13 strike set the stage for the dramatic chain of events that made up the

1920–21 mine war.[19] He goes on to observe, "By 1919–21, state politics had become as meaningless to the miners as had local politics. Even before the Paint Creek–Cabin Creek strike, the miners had questioned a state government that not only allowed the mine-guard system to exist, but that clothed it with state authority."[20] Accordingly, there were two consequences of the strike that proved enduringly relevant. One involved the replacement of UMWA district-level officers with young, local activists who had played a role in the strike. The second was "an explosion of wildcat strikes (that) erupted throughout the Kanawha and New River coal fields.... The wildcat strike was a source of power and a means of imposing their will upon a hostile coal company over issues that touched them most immediately and deeply."[21]

The spark that lit the subsequent mine war came on May 19, 1920, in the Mingo County town of Matewan with the arrival by train of thirteen well-armed guards employed by the Baldwin-Felts Detective Agency. The guards had been dispatched to throw striking miners and their families from the company-owned housing. A group of local residents armed themselves and, under the protection of town sheriff Sid Hatfield and town mayor C.C. Testerman, confronted the Baldwin-Felts agents, and asked them under what authority they could evict strikers. Satisfied that the armed guards were exceeding any lawful authority, Hatfield contacted the sheriff's office in the county seat of Williamson to arrange for arrest warrants. When Hatfield again approached the armed guards, warrants in hand, a gun fight broke out between the locals and the Baldwin-Felts that left seven of the guards, including two Felts brothers, dead, and on the other side, two miners dead and the mayor fatally wounded.[22]

Strike activity in Mingo continued, as well as organizing by UMWA District 17, now operating under local officers like Frank Keeney and Fred Mooney, veterans of the 1912–13 strike and young activists who emerged once the rank and file had turned out the old guard district officials subservient to the union's international office. The miners' cause was further buoyed by a jury acquittal of Sid Hatfield and fifteen others in a murder trial for charges that arose from the battle of Matewan.[23]

The smoldering conflict between workers on one side and coal companies and state authorities on the other exploded yet again when, on August 1, 1921, Keeney and UMWA district officers learned that Hatfield and local unionist Ed Chambers had been ambushed and shot dead by Baldwin-Felts agents on the steps of the McDowell County courthouse in Welch.[24] An estimated crowd of two thousand attended Hatfield's funeral in Matewan. The eulogy offered included words that signaled subsequent events: "There can be no peace in West Virginia until the enforcement of the law is removed from the hands of private detective agencies, and from those of deputy sheriffs who are paid ... by great corporations, most of them owned by nonresidents who have no interest in West Virginia's tomorrow."[25] Practically speaking, the really existing class struggle was at the same time a rebellion against really existing government.

The murder of Hatfield and Chambers was one outrage too many for Keeney and the miners of the southern coalfields. By late August of 1921, hundreds of miners began mobilizing at Lens Creek for a projected armed invasion of antiunion strongholds that began in Logan County and extended south. Wearing red bandanas to distinguish themselves, an army of fifteen to twenty thousand miners marched south, where they were met and engaged in battle by law enforcement and mine guards all along the ridgeline of Blair Mountain in Logan County.[26]

After several days of warfare, by September 1, 1921, the miners' army was poised to descend into Logan when the federal government dispatched federal troops to intervene and disarm the workers, ending the campaign as miners, many of them World War I veterans, were unwilling to engage in battle against American troops.[27] Subsequent jury trials, conducted in Martinsburg, site of the beginning the 1877 general strike, resulted in the acquittal of all but one of the UMWA members formally charged with treason against the state of West Virginia.

Contested Terrain

The rout of the miners' armed march at Blair Mountain by federal military intervention had the obvious consequence of reinforcing the coal industry's dominance over the social, political, and economic life of West Virginia. It also cleared the way for strengthening a highly vertical autocracy within the UMWA. In 1919, John L. Lewis was able to internally assert personal control of the union, as he suppressed radical insurgents from West Virginia westward to Kansas, aided by no lesser a figure than the former agitator Mother Jones.

Lewis's ascendancy within the union was not entirely unprecedented. As president, he was in many regards an official in the image of John Mitchell, a business unionist who was essentially conservative in outlook and, unlike the revolutionary syndicalists, accepted the legitimacy of wage labor as an institutional feature of social relations.[28] Lewis was also in accord with the approach to mechanization that had been taken by Mitchell: the union needed to collaborate with, rather than resist, the introduction of technology into mining. Mechanization, especially in an economic context in which private ownership and competition were unalterable givens, had the practical consequence of undermining workers' control of the productive process by regimenting the pace of work activity, as well as reducing the number of needed employees. These effects all accrued to the benefit of the boss rather than the worker.[29]

As labor historian Keith Dix tells it, Lewis had for a time allowed some room for internal socialist dissidents like John Brophy to argue in favor of the nationalization of mine ownership, as distinct from "the more radical idea of worker ownership of the mines," but this concession was early on, in 1922, during Lewis's rise to autocratic power. What the syndicalist and socialist visions had in common was workplace democracy wherein "coal shall be run by the people who mine it." By 1925 Lewis had cemented his control within the union and could effectively bury even a social democratic notion like nationalization of mine ownership.[30]

Lewis sought to harness the increasing mechanization of coal mining to win higher, union-negotiated wages, sidestepping both workers' control and the effect of massive layoffs. The latter effect had a sustained demographic impact in West Virginia. The extended period in which Blacks from the rural South and immigrants from southern and eastern Europe swelled the coal mining workforce and the state's population—during coal extraction's early rise to dominance—was over time reversed. West Virginians streamed out to destinations such as Michigan, Ohio, and eventually North Carolina as employment in the mines began its long and unrelenting decline.

That decline, however, did not occur all at once, and the march toward mechanization was coincident with the transformation of organized labor that followed upon the New Deal's regime of labor relations that favored, at least temporarily, the growth of labor unions, even when those unions were increasingly and internally autocracies rather than employee-run democratic organizations. Although over time the number of miners needed to extract coal diminished, the side effect of increased dust levels in the mines posed a new and devastating peril. Unmonitored and unregulated coal dust had two dangers. Dust buildup could trigger explosions, as well as permanently harm the health of those who dug the coal.

Despite his iron grip on administrative power within the UMWA, Lewis had his challengers. In West Virginia, Frank Keeney mounted an effort when, on March 16, 1931, he helped organize the West Virginia Mine Workers, which, within two months, had recruited twenty-three thousand members, and by July had led a strike of seventeen thousand in the southern coalfields of the state. In this he was opposed by another veteran of the Blair Mountain march, William Blizzard, who had made peace with Lewis and actively sought to combat the rise of the insurgent union. The realities of the Depression era, the violent opposition of the UMWA and the State Federation of Labor, and the arrival of the New Deal's National Industrial Recovery Act all combined to render the new union untenable and it dissolved in June 1933.[31]

Lewis maintained his control of the UMWA for four decades, finally retiring in 1960. His replacement Tom Kennedy died in 1963 and was replaced by the vice president, Tony Boyle, who had once, long ago, made a reputation by crusading for mine safety in Montana.[32] Employment in mining continued its decline until 1963, and then began to slowly increase as demand and production rose. Paul Nyden draws a direct connection between the economic recovery in coal and the reemergence of rank-and-file militancy.[33] Whatever the explanation, the number and frequency of wildcat strikes by miners steadily rose throughout the 1960s.

Boyle not only benefited from the autocratic structure that Lewis had established, he also continued in the spirit of Lewis's insistence that the interests of the coal industry and the interests of its employees were fundamentally in alignment. Just after November 20, 1968, when Consolidation Coal Company's Farmington No. 9 mine exploded, killing seventy-eight miners, Boyle praised the corporation as "one of the best companies to work with so far as cooperation and safety are concerned," and downplayed the disaster by saying, "As long as we mine coal, there is always this inherent danger."[34] An in-depth investigation of the Farmington operation, however, reveals that Consolidation's operation was plagued with buildups in coal dust and methane, and that a safety alarm of a ventilation fan had been deactivated. The explosion and massive death toll had been entirely preventable.[35]

It could be argued, as has been, that Boyle's autocratic regime, committed to accommodation and "business" unionism, was unconcerned, and even ill equipped, to deal with the working membership's safety imperatives, much less "questions concerning control over the technology and the work process." Those matters had been contractually ceded to management.[36]

In the wake of Farmington, a grassroots movement aided by a number of coalfield doctors began to emerge around the prevalence of black lung disease that afflicted and disabled coal miners. In West Virginia this was manifested in the formation of the Black Lung Association. By January 26, 1969, the demand for addressing what was a severe public health crisis mobilized a meeting of three thousand miners in Charleston that condemned the inaction of the UMWA hierarchy under Boyle and proposed major compensation and legal reforms. By February 10, 1969, wildcat strikes began throughout the state, and hundreds of striking miners flooded the state capitol the next day just as legislative hearings on pending bills took place.

When days passed after the massive protest with no apparent progress on black lung, striking resumed on February 19, 1969. It was reported that roving pickets closed mines in the state's southern counties involving as many as twelve thousand workers. On February 26, with the strike spreading throughout West Virginia, three thousand protesters turned up at the state capitol, and by the beginning of March, forty-five thousand coal miners were on strike. After twenty-three days of strikes, Governor Arch Moore signed a compromise version of black lung compensation into law on March 11.[37] It was widely agreed that the black lung insurgency was not only a rebellion against the coal industry's political dominance of the government, it was also a rejection of the Boyle hierarchy. The discontent within the ranks emboldened one long-time union bureaucrat, Jock Yablonski of western Pennsylvania, to mount a challenge to Boyle's hold on the union presidency on May 29, 1969. Yablonski calculated that an attack on Boyle's corruption and his suppression of internal democracy, as well as Boyle's neglect of health and safety, would win Yablonski the support of the union's rank and file in a challenge for union presidency.[38]

Although on December 9, 1969, the official election vote tally for UMWA president went decidedly against Yablonski, assassins hired by Boyle entered the Yablonski home on December 31 and murdered the Yablonski family as they slept. Only then did the federal government respond to charges of a rigged election, and it would be two years before a new election was ordered. At Yablonski's funeral, coal miners in attendance founded a new organization, Miners for Democracy, setting in motion a movement to reclaim the UMWA for its rank and file.[39]

It was with this history and in this context that the first significant public workers strike in West Virginia history, the 1969 state road strike, was situated.

CHAPTER 2

1969–1979

State Road Strike 1969

Judging by an official history published in 1960 by the State Federation of Labor, the AFL-affiliated unions had up to that point paid scant attention to public workers in West Virginia at the county and state levels. Despite the founding of a state affiliate to the American Federation of Teachers (AFT) in 1935, as late as 1953 not a single AFT local existed in West Virginia.[1] In 1953, the only chartered local for the American Federation of State, County and Municipal Employees (AFSCME) was among correctional officers at the state penitentiary in Moundsville.[2]

One of the earliest and largest job actions among public workers in West Virginia took place in 1969, soon after an outgoing Democratic governor, Hulett Smith, was succeeded by Republican candidate Arch Moore. The long-established practice had been in the form of the "spoils" system: certain jobs, including those of maintenance employees working for the State Road Commission, were contingent on whomever won electoral office. The successful candidates—or party, faction, or machine—would fill existing state jobs with functionaries and workers drawn from the ranks of their supporters and politically connected individuals who would then displace incumbent job holders.[3]

This practice was left over from the patronage or crony system that prevailed in the early period of governance in America, from the days before civil service, reminiscent of a time when political fixers could routinely distribute cash—or even containers of alcohol—at the polls. Political machine bosses could deliver votes (as was often said in West Virginia) for "a dollar and a swaller."

The rampant corruption of the spoils system became increasingly discredited throughout the early twentieth century, making it less and less acceptable for a new governor to engage in wholesale job replacement upon winning office. Still, given the longstanding tradition, and Arch Moore's political reputation, expectations of a purge among state road employees was very much in evidence in 1969.

Just prior to the election of the new governor, the Laborers' International Union of North America, AFL-CIO, began signing up state highway workers, despite the lack of any legal provision for public sector collective bargaining. This effort seemed to have been especially effective in West Virginia's southern counties, where the tradition of UMWA rank-and-file militancy was being reinvigorated by the insurgent Black Lung Association, as well as what would subsequently become the successful, insurgent Miners for Democracy.[4]

The Laborers' Union began organizing state road employees around a number of concrete issues such as conditions of public employment, which included seniority, wrongful discharge and discipline, and grievance rights. According to a federal judicial court memorandum decision, between August 24, 1968, and March 1, 1969, approximately four thousand employees of the State Road Commission had signed union membership authorization cards.[5]

The incoming governor—who later became a convicted felon—was restrained to some degree by public opinion and by the fact that at least some state jobs had already been removed from the patronage-spoils system by the incremental encroachment of civil service reforms that had begun in selected West Virginia state agencies in 1960. On February 6, 1969, the union met with the new governor's administrator of state roads to discuss the terms and conditions of employment of the "substantial majority" of state road employees, now represented by the Laborers' Union. There were to all accounts no tangible results from that initial attempt to engage in negotiation.[6]

On February 10, 1969, the Laborers' Union informed the State Road Commission administrator that the union "had been besieged by calls from state road employees to the effect that large-scale replacements were to take place on Monday, February 17." This expectation was apparently widespread, although Moore had on October 30, 1968, a month prior to his election, "indicated that he did not anticipate discharging jobholders merely for political expediency." Nevertheless, "the fear of discharge persisted among the Commission employees." As a consequence, the commissioner reportedly notified the union that fears of mass firings were unfounded and that Moore had no intention "to make any large-scale replacement of Commission employees."[7]

Verbal assurances notwithstanding, rumors and anticipation of mass firings continued to persist. On February 24, 1969, the union informed the commissioner that State Road Commission employees "were becoming increasingly concerned about their job security as well as other grievances and that a walkout might be immanent." Despite this communication, no further response, comments, or assurances addressing those concerns were forthcoming from the new administration.[8]

On March 3, 1969, the newly organized highway equipment operators went out on what Moore described as an illegal strike. The workers demanded union recognition for the purposes of gaining seniority rights and job security. It was clear that by raising an issue of job security in the context of the emerging dispute, highway workers were intent on contesting their "at-will" status as the prevailing, and presumptively controlling, condition of their continued employment.

A week after the walkout began, heavy snowfall blanketed many parts of the state, creating widespread hazardous driving conditions that Moore declared to be an "emergency" situation, and he ordered the strikers back to work so that roads could be cleared. His return-to-work order having been largely ignored, on March 11, 1969, the governor summarily fired all those who had refused the order. In what was arguably an attempt to distance himself from any public perception that he was playing the scab, Moore explicitly stated that he was not dismissing the strikers for engaging in union activity.[9]

On March 14, 1969, striking road workers marched in a mass protest on the governor's office at the state capitol. On March 27, Moore announced that 530 of the strikers had returned to work, as ordered, and that 2,097 state road workers were officially dismissed from the agency for having failed to return to work. He additionally claimed that 1,164 replacement workers had been hired to clear and maintain roadways.[10] At the time, it was reported that many of the fired strikers had sought and found work in the then-booming coal industry, especially in the southern counties where pro-union sentiment ran high. Nevertheless, an estimated 1,500 union members again marched on the state capitol to protest the firings on April 7.

The Laborers' Union subsequently challenged the legality of the governor's dismissal of striking state highway workers in US district court. According to that legal action, the mass firing was construed as a violation of the state's constitution and law because the dismissals were based on the workers' union affiliation and activity, and that, as such, it contravened their rights to petition the government for the redress of grievances, and to exercise their rights to freedom of speech and association. Furthermore, the union claimed that the dismissals aimed to uphold a spoils system of political patronage; that the state had arbitrarily and unreasonably refused to meet and confer with the strikers; and that it violated due process insofar as proper notice, specific charges, and a hearing had been denied to the strikers prior to the dismissals.[11]

The legal challenge sought relief in the form of a reversal of the firings, a $250,000 judgment for damages, the restoration of back pay, an injunction requiring the state to meet and confer with employees, and an injunction prohibiting any discrimination in employment on the basis of union or political affiliation.[12]

In a memorandum opinion, issued January 12, 1970, the federal court ruled that "the dispositive issue is whether the plaintiffs had a right to engage in a strike against the State of West Virginia under either federal or state law." The court contended that while the courts had previously ruled that public workers had a right to union membership, there was no federal or state recognition of either the right of public workers to strike or the right of government employees to bargain collectively.[13]

The Laborers' Union countered with an argument that there was neither a clear statutory provision in West Virginia prohibiting public employee strikes nor any clear ruling by the state's Supreme Court of Appeals that addressed the matter. The federal court sidestepped the union's argument by what it admitted to be a "somewhat novel argument" that the state's constitution gave deference to common law in undecided matters, and that it was "axiomatic that a strike by public employees for any purpose is illegal under the common law, and no statutory declaration of their illegality is necessary." The federal court went on to cite a 1949 Ohio ruling that asserted that any public workers strike was "a rebellion against government."[14]

The federal court concluded that the state had both the discretion and the responsibility to terminate the employment of striking public workers. Noting what the court designated as the strikers' "misconduct," the court further concluded that the workers had no right to continued employment as they "were employed in a classification which was not covered by the West Virginia Civil Service Act and accordingly they had no job tenure under the law of this State. Their argument that this exclusion from the Civil Service statute violates the equal protection clause of the 14th amendment has been rejected in a number of cases."[15] Essentially, the federal district that ruled against the state road workers in *Kirker* reaffirmed the lingering and ongoing patronage system within West Virginia's public sector by upholding the at-will doctrine for the dismissal of state employees when the court concluded that those who "live by the political sword must be prepared to die by the political sword."[16]

It would in no way diminish the efforts of the Laborers' Union in organizing highway maintenance employees in 1969 to acknowledge that the actual catalyst of the strike itself was the widely shared perception by state road workers that Moore was intent on following a long-established convention of replacing existing personnel with politically connected employees of his own choosing. Presumptively, some of them may have originally gained their jobs in just such a manner. Simply saying that those who live by the political sword must also die by the political sword—or that the former beneficiaries of Democratic patronage must passively accept the ascendancy of Republican patronage—does little to ameliorate or justify the corrupting effects of the spoils system.

It would be understandable to conclude that the 1969 state road strike was a complete failure. That appraisal, however, ignores a few relevant considerations. Employees of the State Road Commission, eventually realigned as employees of the West Virginia Division of Highways (DOH), came to be subject to fuller civil service protections and, as a result, to a requirement of "for-cause" disciplinary action. While the historical residue of political patronage lingered in highway employment long after 1969, it was met by repeated and occasionally successful challenges.[17]

The 1969 highway strike exhibited a number of recurring features of public worker insurgency. The presence or intervention of an established business union was frequently a factor in provoking—as well as providing a vehicle for—preexisting worker discontent and grievance. Yet that organizational presence proved incapable of containing and directing the expression of that discontent. The admitted failure of the state road strike also turned out to be a precondition for eventual political and legal reforms that, although they often left the underlying demand for meaningful worker power unrealized, brought about substantial and enduring improvements in working conditions for state employees. The struggle also paved the way for subsequent and more radical eruptions of insurgency. Though limited and to all appearances defeated, the 1969 state road strike pointed in the direction of future struggles that would be undertaken by West Virginian public workers.

West Virginia Public Employees Association

Discontent on the part of state employees during the first term of Arch Moore was by no means limited to employees of the State Road Commission. The Moore administration's autocratic disregard for state workers proved to be a catalyst for the creation of the West Virginia Public Employees Association (WVPEA) on August 30, 1971.

WVPEA was self-consciously "independent" and modeled on state civil service and state public employee associations that flourished elsewhere leading up to that time. One of its principal issues was state workers' continued "enslavement to the spoils-partisan-patronage system" coupled to the goal of "the development of West Virginia as a progressive state." WVPEA also explicitly linked improvements in the civil service system to improved pay and working conditions and the elimination of the rampant practice of retaliation that characterized Moore's administration.[18]

The association was explicitly geared in much of its activity toward electoral action as a means to achieve full-blown civil service law for West Virginia state government. As it turned out, a comprehensive enactment of civil service law modeled on the federal system was not to be fully and finally implemented in West Virginia until 1989, twenty years after the state road strike.[19] Meanwhile, however, the association saw little reason to compromise or to endorse the positions on civil service of either Moore or Jay Rockefeller, the competing standard-bearers for the state's Republican and Democratic parties. However much electoral action by workers has frequently devolved to choosing the "lesser evil" in American two-party politics, WVPEA seemed to have been somewhat willing to adopt a "plague on both your houses" stance when it came to executive branch administrations.

In 1972, for example, WVPEA again affirmed that its top legislative priority would be the improvement of civil service in West Virginia state government in a version that aligned with failed senate bills that had been introduced earlier that year in regular session, modeled on the creation of a Civil Service Commission. The association's president at that time was Herbert Wilcox, an associate professor at West Virginia University who would be succeeded that same year by Julius McLeod, an associate professor in social work at the historically Black West Virginia State College. Wilcox was explicitly critical of state government at the time as being a continuation of the spoils system with a veneer of civil service law as no more than "cosmetic frosting."[20] Other legislative goals for WVPEA at the time were higher wages and improved working conditions and the implementation of a "meet and confer" arrangement for negotiating by which WVPEA could "engage in collective bargaining in a restricted sense or within the limits of the law governing public employees."[21]

Despite an imputed reference to collective bargaining, Wilcox was at pains to distinguish the proposed legislation of the WVPEA from competing bills that had been introduced on behalf of the West Virginia Labor Federation of the AFL-CIO and the West Virginia Education Association (WVEA). Affirming the political neutrality of his group, Wilcox described the West Virginia Labor Federation and WVEA bills as establishing a basis for politicized unionization and the "fragmentation of employee representation," with rival unions fighting to determine proprietary jurisdiction for bargaining units, as well as potentially generating "adversarial" relations between low-level managers and their subordinates. Nevertheless, WVPEA advocated the creation of a grievance procedure along a revamping of civil service and indicated that such reforms might be expanded to include city and county government units.[22]

Although its own political effectiveness proved to be negligible, WVPEA as an organization did establish a number of chapters, including Huntington, centered in the state hospital; Mason County, centered at Lakin state nursing home; one at the Colin Anderson Center; and another in Raleigh County. Each of these communities were tethered more or less to the presence of state-operated health facilities. WVPEA bemoaned the difficulty of signing up members in the state capitol of Charleston due to an evident "fear of reprisals and harassment" that association organizers had reportedly encountered during leafleting at the state capitol complex.[23]

WVPEA exhibited an indecisive hesitation—if not an outright ambivalence—in situating its programs and proposals between conflicting goals, some of which were traditionally identified as typical of "professional" associations and some of which were demands historically pushed forward by labor unions. Aside from the standard issues perennially afflicting public workers in West Virginia—inadequate pay being the most commonplace—WVPEA was willing to also contest a number of agency-specific issues, such as the Division of Vocational Rehabilitation's imposition of an arbitrary dress code, which included proscribed hairstyles and detailed requirements of clothing fashion that were, by 1971 cultural standards, an easy target for mockery and ridicule. As it turned out, it would not be the last time public workers organized workplace resistance around "dress codes" forced upon overworked and underpaid state employees, suggesting that—however trivial or superficial such a matter might ordinarily seem—it was nevertheless a tangible measure in the struggle for power in the everyday workplace.

Charleston City Sanitation Strike

In 1970, 220 Charleston city sanitation workers belonging to Local 1548 of the American Federation of State, County and Municipal Employees staged a one-week strike.[24] In 1971, John Hutchinson, a Democrat, became the mayor of Charleston, and in response to a preelection questionnaire, stated that he favored the right of public employees to organize and collectively bargain. Once in office, however, Hutchinson took the extraordinary step of "unilaterally" abolishing the municipal employee civil service system.[25]

AFSCME was chartered by the AFL in 1936 and had originated with the Wisconsin State Administrative Employees Association, which was briefly affiliated with the AFL's federal workers union, the American Federation of Government Employees (AFGE). Once chartered as a stand-alone organization, AFSCME experienced steady growth, starting from 5,355 members that year to more than 200,000 by 1961.[26] From its inception in 1936, AFSCME had supported the idea of collective bargaining for public employees, although its longtime president, Arnold Zander, was careful to distance the union from advocating strikes by public employees.[27]

Len De Caux observes that it was in the heyday of the 1930s New Deal that the AFL—with roots in craft unions and long-oriented toward a conservative, "business unionism" approach—eclipsed remnants of more radical union alternatives, including the revolutionary syndicalists of the Industrial Workers of the World. Yet it was at this very juncture that the United Mine Workers of America (UMWA) spearheaded the formation within the AFL ranks of a response to a growing demand of workers for something capable of operating beyond the narrow confines of craft guilds.[28]

After the formation of the Committee for Industrial Organization (CIO) on November 9, 1935, that organization quickly evolved into "an increasingly autonomous institutional" entity within its AFL "parent" body.[29] CIO organizers like John Brophy and Rose Pesotta were soon involved in efforts targeting the spontaneous demand for unions in such industries as rubber, auto, and steel, to the evident dismay of the AFL old guard.[30] The 1937 expulsion of the CIO from the AFL made manifest the conservative federation's rejection of resurgent worker-driven militancy. In the wake of that expulsion, the CIO, now renamed the Congress of Industrial Organizations, chartered two public sector unions to rival the existing AFL affiliates of AFSCME and the American Federation of Government Employees (AFGE). These CIO affiliates would, in 1946, merge with dissident locals from the AFT to form the United Public Workers of America (UPWA). Throughout its iterations, however, the CIO public sector organization was quite similar to AFSCME, committed to expansion of civil service and the merit system.[31] In the wake of the anticommunist purge among CIO unions, UPWA folded, leaving AFSCME as the only surviving national union for state and local government employees.

Despite the ubiquity of nonstrike provisions in the constitutions of public sector unions after the 1919 Boston police strike, during the 1960s there was a spike in public sector strikes in the United States, which coincided with and paralleled the eruption of wildcat coal strikes in West Virginia. In 1973, James O'Connor noted:

> State unions also have become more militant in their demands for better pay, shorter hours, and better working conditions. Thirty years ago not one state employee

> organization had a strike policy; even unions affiliated with the AFL or the CIO had no-strike provisions in their constitutions. Today the situation is very different. Government unions have called more strikes, which have lasted for longer periods and have involved more workers. In 1953, there were only thirty strikes against state and local governments; in 1966 and 1967, there were 152 and 181 strikes, respectively. During the quarter century prior to 1966, only 129 teachers' strikes were recorded; in 1966, there were 33. In 1967–1968, the AFT alone conducted 32 major walkouts and mini-strikes involving nearly 100,000 workers. In March 1970, 200,000 postal workers went on strike, and during that year and the next dozens of cities and towns were hit by major and minor strikes of municipal workers.[32]

O'Connor gave his account of the national upsurge in public sector strikes in reference to his description of, and explanation for, the social development of what had come to be termed as "late" or "monopoly" capitalism. The class society defined by capitalist relations not only produced greater and greater inequality in wealth, the capitalist control of the state had led to the adoption of laws and policies that socialized the costs of capitalist reproduction—such as environmental clean-up, the legal defense of indigent defendants, social services for the working poor and the unemployed, etc.—it also sought to privatize and profit from the state sector by contracting out highway building and maintenance, relying on private prisons and security and for-profit delivery of social services, and so forth. Coupled with extreme inequities in taxation and the allocation of state sector funding, those trends gave rise to what O'Connor designated as the "fiscal crisis of the state."[33]

O'Connor concluded,

> The growth of unionism and rank-and-file militancy is attributable to a number of factors ... but the main reasons spring from the fiscal crisis itself. State employees (and dependents and clients) increasingly are aware that they are subject to

> a gradual erosion of material standards because of budgetary priorities that favor social investment, the tax revolt, inflation, and state policies designed to restrain inflation. Most strikes are called over wage demands (which cannot be linked to rising profits). The fiscal crisis also subjects state workers (and clients) to profound qualitative changes in their relations with state administrators and politicians. Workers and administrators thus are engaged in both quantitative and qualitative struggles which interpenetrate at nearly every point in the state sector.... In brief, the social meaning of the fiscal crisis goes well beyond immediate budgetary issues.[34]

By way of conclusion, O'Connor enumerated factors in the rising politicization and radicalization of public workers that had begun in the 1960s, again with reference to the 1970 postal strike, and noted,

> There is the illegality, the unwillingness of state administrators to bargain in good faith, and the state's easy access to injunctions against picketing of state facilities: These conditions force state employee unions to think in terms of a whole range of political issues—the right to organize, the right to strike, freedom of assembly, freedom of speech, and so on. Thus, for example, the postal workers' strike necessarily forced the workers to organize themselves and to avoid reliance on either the good will of state administrators or the union officials. The first national-level wildcat strike in US history, it may have ushered in a period of worker action independent of trade unions.[35]

As a union, AFSCME was initially unwilling to either embrace organizing Black municipal sanitation workers or extend support whenever they went on strike on their own initiative, as those workers did in Philadelphia and Atlanta during the late 1930s and 1940s.[36] After the spontaneous 1951 sanitation workers strike in Birmingham, and a 1959 sit-down strike in Charlotte, and a Miami "unauthorized" walkout the same year, AFSCME began a realignment similar to the initial CIO recognition in the 1930s that it was either get on board or be left stranded at the station.[37]

The trajectory of that realignment came not during Zander's tenure, but rather during the union presidency of Jerry Wurf. Hired as an organizer by Zander in 1947, Jerry Wurf took AFSCME's New York District Council 37 from six hundred members to more than twenty thousand by the early 1960s, using a mechanism for collective bargaining by exclusive representation that was based on the prevailing model ushered in during the New Deal for private sector unions.[38] By 1964, Wurf had replaced Zander as the union's international president.[39] Nevertheless, it was not until 1968 that AFSCME would forge a working alliance with the Southern Christian Leadership Conference and, at the same time, throw organizational backing behind mainly southern Black municipal sanitation workers who were spontaneously initiating strikes.[40] In the words of W.T. Jones, "While AFSCME continued to focus on white-collar civil servants, it was the militancy of African-American laborers that drove the discussion about public employee unionism in the South."[41]

Joseph Hower draws attention to a parallel between the CIO's embrace of militant industrial organizing and the later convergence of AFSCME with the civil rights movement: "Like John L. Lewis and the industrial union movement of the 1930s, Wurf neither created the movement nor caused the surge in public sector militancy. He was as much a creature as creator of the 'the new world of trade unionism,' his influence relied on the individual and collective actions of millions of rank-and-file workers and local activists, and his successes (and failures) owed as much to broader, uncontrollable elements of the political and social landscape as they did to his own decisions and actions."[42]

The momentous 1968 Memphis sanitation strike by AFSCME Local 1733, during which Dr. Martin Luther King Jr. was assassinated, was still undoubtedly in the national consciousness when, on July 31, 1972, 150 Charleston city workers belonging to AFSCME Local 1548 walked off the job demanding union recognition and a written grievance procedure.[43] Although there already were negotiated agreements between public agencies—including West Virginia University and the cities of Fairmont and Huntington—and employees in West Virginia at the time, and no statutes prohibiting them in state law, Charleston's Democratic mayor, John Hutchinson justified his intransigence by insisting that any negotiation for public employee collective bargaining was illegal. He did not, however, go so far as saying that public workers were prohibited from forming or joining a union organization. Led by city incinerator worker and Local 1548 president Hollie Brown, the initial strikers were mainly from municipal units of the incinerator, street department, civic center, and sanitary board, and there was a complete cessation of city garbage pickup. Brown stated that 70 percent of city workers were in the union, although he noted that the city had not been properly withholding union dues from members' paychecks.[44]

According to Brown, the mainly Black incinerator employees and mainly white street department were at the forefront of the strike and exhibited complete solidarity in staging the walkout. It is worth noting that Brown, from the coal mining community of Cabin Creek, had worked as a miner for a time and had narrowly survived a roof fall when working underground because of the intervention of a white fellow miner. His father had been a long-time coal miner and dedicated union member, his family having been brought to West Virginia from Alabama by the coal company to serve as strikebreakers, but they had joined the UMWA instead of scabbing.[45]

Critics on the city council pointed out that the mayor had already "unilaterally" abolished the civil service system for city employees, although it was later revealed that in response to a preelection questionnaire, Hutchinson had stated that he favored the right of public employees to organize and collectively bargain. By August 3, 1972, Hutchinson issued "Red Man" warrants for Brown, Leroy Easly, and Jimmy Harris.[46]

On August 5, 1972, the city announced that it had abandoned seeking a temporary court order against the strike but would begin legal action for a permanent injunction. Local 1548 president Brown disclosed that he had only informed the AFSCME international office of the walkout, a pattern already exhibited in Memphis and Philadelphia, after the strike had been locally approved and initiated.[47] Two days later came the revelation that, in response to a preelection questionnaire, Hutchinson had stated that he favored the right of public employees to organize and collectively bargain.

On August 8, 1972, Hutchinson publicly declared it was the last chance for city strikers to return to work or they would be fired effective August 24. Local president Brown had already received a letter stating that he was going to be dismissed. Again, Hutchinson referred to the strike as an "illegal work stoppage."[48] On August 9, Brown was arrested by city police for assault and public intoxication, although he was a nondrinker, and two other strikers were arrested for picketing the municipal Civic Center.[49] It was later disclosed that undercover city police were assigned to shadow strikers and that several unmarked rental vehicles were used by city police to follow and surveil striking workers in order to find a pretext to arrest them.[50]

On August 10, 1972, city firefighters joined the picket lines. The Kanawha Valley Labor Council had already voted to support the strike. On September 19, Hutchinson cited the 1969 federal court decision against state road strikers, as well as a ruling from former state attorney general C. Donald Robertson, as evidence that public employee collective bargaining was illegal in West Virginia.[51] On September 25, Rev. Ron English of the Charleston Black Ministerial Alliance announced there would be a rally in support of the striking city workers and that Southern Council Leadership Conference president Ralph Abernathy would attend.[52] The next day, Abernathy joined a march and rally of an estimated 700 people in support of the striking municipal workers, those in attendance carrying signs that simply said "Dignity."[53]

On September 28, 1972, despite Abernathy's defiant declaration in Charleston that "we were born under injunction," the strikers were hit by a permanent injunction barring picketing that had been sought by Hutchinson in Kanawha County Circuit Court. Judge Frank Taylor, quoting the decision in *Kirker* (which in turn had quoted *Amalgamated Association of Street, Electric Railway and Motorcoach Employees of America*) "held that the strike was a 'rebellion against government,'"[54] The charge, made by city officials during the 1968 Memphis strike, that striking city sanitation workers constituted a de facto "threat of anarchy" was essentially repeated.[55]

The next day the strikers announced that they would honor the circuit court injunction banning picketing but that they would continue the strike. Brown told the press, "We came out 80 days ago for dignity. That hasn't changed. We're still striking the city for recognition, a fair grievance procedure, and a return to work without reprisals." Strikers also planned to march to the local welfare office on Monday in order to seek benefits. At the last report of that date, fifty-two strikers had already been fired, with another group of one hundred having receiving letters ordering them to report to work.[56]

On October 3, 1972, the newspaper reported that a "resolution that would have put fifty-two fired city workers back on the payroll and under the civil service ordinance ended in a tie vote during Monday's meeting of Charleston City Council.... Consequently, the measure was defeated." The resolution would have established a grievance board, recognized the union, and allowed the return to work of all strikers without reprisal. The mayor agreed to reestablish the city Civil Service Commission and the resolution's backer, 18th Ward council member Jack Bennett voted to table the motion in exchange. Then Bennett made another motion to reemploy fired strikers allowing any disciplinary charges against them to be filed with and handled by the Civil Service Commission. Council member Robert Crawford questioned the reason for rehire. At-large member Virgil Matthews replied that rehiring was necessary so that, if appropriate, charges could be brought in a proper forum. The city's Civil Service Commission had previously announced it was dropping a state supreme court appeal. Hutchinson then argued that charges had already been brought and would be heard before the commission. Council member at-large Kent Hall answered that anyone off the job for fifteen days lost the right to appeal. "Bennett, trying to garner council support, said he wouldn't submit a motion if he didn't believe the city was as responsible for the long walkout as were the strikers who left their jobs illegally." Bennett had conducted an investigation into the causes of the strike and told the council that the harassment of street and incinerator workers had gone on for years, and stated, "You would have reacted the same way if you had been treated as those men have been." Council member Joe Smith stated that the mayor's closing of the incinerator and switching to curbside garbage bag pickup had eliminated fifty jobs. Several in attendance proposed rehiring strikers, then laying them off in accordance with civil service procedure.[57]

In a separate report on October 3, 1972, Bennett confirmed to journalists that "Hutchinson agreed to withdraw his Civil Service Commission appeal in exchange for Bennett's promise that he'd neither introduce nor support an ordinance and resolution pertaining to the city strike." Virgil Matthews contended that the mayor didn't give up anything in the deal, and that "the State Supreme Court would have upheld the validity of the Civil Service ordinance." Bennett told the reporter, "I walked into the mayor's office and he surprised me by offering to drop the appeal and provide civil service coverage to all city workers. I gave up my vote to get Civil Service back."[58] Bennett tried to also convince Hutchinson to rehire the fired workers, but the mayor refused.[59] Early Monday, a march was held to the Kanawha County Department of Welfare in order to sign strikers up for benefits.[60]

On October 6, 1972, the city newspaper published a lengthy interview between Thomas J. Gagliardo, public affairs representative from the international office of AFSCME, and *Charleston Gazette* publisher Ned Chilton, as well as editors Harry Hoffman and L.T. Anderson. A student at Catholic University School of Law, Gagliardo had been in Charleston for two months assisting Local 1548 in public outreach and community support. Gagliardo noted that on the previous day, forty-one area college professors expressed support for city workers because their struggle would benefit the public "by removing patronage hiring and ... stabilizing the workforce of the city." Such strike demands resulted in more productive, trained, and experienced workers and increased productivity. Government officials, who tended to become biased bosses, could be compelled by the union to adhere to objective rather than arbitrary standards.[61]

When Anderson raised the prospect of a general strike of public workers and concluded that it would have chaotic consequences, Gagliardo replied that was "all the more reason to treat public employees more fairly." Gagliardo went on to cite public workers' right to strike in Sweden, Britain, France, Germany, and Italy: "It's not entirely bad. The strike is the last resort." Gagliardo then condemned public jobs as a "political plum" that allowed politicians "to fire thousands of people and hire new people." When Chilton countered that "those days are pretty well gone forever," Gagliardo observed that "Arch Moore did it only a couple of years ago." He also contrasted that action with a state road strike in Pennsylvania eighteen month prior.[62]

Gagliardo stated, "There are more strikes in states without repressive anti-strike laws.... What causes strikes is injustice. What prevents strikes is justice.... The workers in Charleston came to us and said we've tried everything else, we've approached the mayor, we tried every angle and we've decided to go out on strike. That was the expression of the democratic rule of the local union." Gagliardo pointed out that Hutchinson shut down the incinerator, a $1.6 million investment, rented as many as eighteen cars without city council approval to conduct strike breaking activities, bought garbage bags to dispense without city council approval, and hired the antiunion law firm Jackson, Kelly, Holt, and O'Farrell to seek injunctions and court rulings at substantial expense.[63]

On October 13, 1972, Operation Human Dignity staged a march on city hall led by Rev. Ronald English. In a written reply sent to the marchers by Hutchinson, the mayor "said he has never questioned any man's dignity. However, he reiterated his position that the strike and any collective bargaining agreement would be a violation of the law. He said he agreed that employees are entitled to a grievance procedure and for that reason he requested that the city Civil Service Commission withdraw its appeal to the state supreme court. Hutchinson suggested the men seek redress through that body." Marchers occupied the city conference room, with police scattered throughout city hall, but there were no anticipated arrests.[64] It was announced that Rev. Ralph Abernathy would return to Charleston on Sunday to lead further protests.[65]

Miners for Democracy candidate Arnold Miller, having been declared the winner of the UMWA presidential election, came to Charleston and conducted a press conference with AFSCME's Jerry Wurf and expressed his support for the city sanitation strike and for public employee collective bargaining legislation in West Virginia.[66] Nevertheless, AFSCME's inability to overturn the injunction on picketing hobbled the sanitation strike going forward, and it was finally declared to be over by the union when strike pay was ended in May 1973.[67]

Public Hospital Workers

The hospital workers' union Local 1199 began in 1932, organizing among New York City drugstores and by 1938 was part of the formation of the Retail, Wholesale and Department Store Union (RWDSU) under the auspices of the CIO. Like many unions of the period, 1199 was openly leftist and militant and eventually began successfully organizing among hospital workers, aided in that venture by its politically progressive and antiracist approach.[68]

By 1969, Local 1199 had set its sights on expanding outside of New York, and a bitter and hard-fought hospital strike in Charleston, South Carolina, signaled that commitment. That year, Local 1199 also set up an organizational branch in Pennsylvania. In 1970, a branch was established in West Virginia, followed by one in Ohio in 1971, and another in Virginia in 1972. Although it retained its affiliation with RWDSU, 1199 internally reorganized as the National Union of Hospital and Health Care Employees (NUHHCE) in November 1973, reflective of the union's growing membership in the health care industry. As a newly minted national union, 1199 continued its practice of establishing state branches, creating yet another one in Kentucky in 1975.

NUHHCE also hired organizing staff to service and help administer the new branches. One of the union staff members hired in 1974 was a local West Virginia activist named Tom Woodruff.[69] One of Woodruff's earliest efforts in Local 1199 involved the organization of hospital workers at the public sector Cabell Huntington Hospital near the Marshall University main campus, which resulted in winning a collective bargaining contract with a major public employer.[70]

Woodruff was also a staff representative on a collective bargaining agreement with 1199's partner and affiliate organization, RWDSU Local 550, when it signed a contract for maintenance workers at another municipal public sector facility, Fairmont General Hospital, owned and operated by the City of Fairmont. In the contract that went into effect on March 2, 1977, Local 550 agreed to not expand the covered bargaining unit at Fairmont General for the duration of the contract.[71]

In August 1978, nursing staff at Fairmont General decided to organize under the auspices of Local 1199, and hospital administrators took the position that Woodruff's dual representational role on behalf of Locals 550 and 1199 constituted a de facto violation of its contract with RWDSU Local 550. On September 11, 1978, the nurses of Fairmont General went on strike to support their demand for recognition of Local 1199 as their designated bargaining agent.

> Correspondence and telegrams were exchanged between the hospital and Mr. Woodruff, and it was the latter's position that the nurses were being represented by Local 1199 of the Hospital and Health Care Union. Several nurses, together with Mr. Woodruff, made abortive attempts to discuss the union's representation with the hospital administration staff and to present to the hospital management a petition signed by 156 nurses affirming their desire to have Local 1199 act as their bargaining agent. When the hospital refused to meet with nursing representatives and Mr. Woodruff, it

was advised that by a vote of 145 to 9 the nurses and other technical employees would on September 11, 1978, refuse to work.[72]

The City of Fairmont sought an injunction in Marion County Circuit Court for what administrators described as an "illegal" nurses' strike. When this was refused by the county court, the legal action was amended to recover financial damages arising from the nurses' walkout. After the circuit court refused to award damages against either RWDSU Local 550 or Local 1199, the case was appealed by the city to the West Virginia Supreme Court of Appeals.[73]

Justice Thomas Miller delivered the court's decision that "while some constitutional protection is extended under the First Amendment to public employees to organize, speak freely and petition, it is clear that a public employer is not required to recognize or bargain with a public employee association or union in the absence of a statutory requirement." This latter feature, given the continued failure of the West Virginia legislature to pass a law addressing public sector collective bargaining nevertheless indicated how West Virginia differed from other southern states, such as Virginia and North Carolina, which had passed provisions specifically prohibiting all public collective bargaining. In *City of Fairmont*, the court noted that there was little precedent as to "whether a common law cause of action exists for damages arising from a peaceful work stoppage against the employer by public employees." Rejecting the employers contention that, for the purposes of common law, the strike for recognition by 1199 members was in any way illegal, the court concluded "that where public employees who have no employment contracts with their employer, engage in a work stoppage which is peaceful and directed only against the employer with no attempt to interfere with his customers or bar ingress to other employees there is no common law right to damages."[74]

In a separate, concurring opinion, Justice Darrell McGraw stated the matter more forcibly:

> Public employees, as a class, have a constitutionally protected right under the First Amendment to the United States Constitution, as do other first class citizens, to associate with others in a labor organization whose purpose is to attempt to negotiate terms and conditions of employment with their employer.... The rights of speech, association and assembly intertwine in the union context. If "membership" is the aggregate expression of those rights, then membership is likewise protected. "The guarantee of the right of assembly protects more than the right to attend a meeting but also includes the right to express one's attitude or philosophies by membership in a group or by affiliation with it or by other lawful means."[75]

Going beyond the analysis offered by Miller, McGraw wrote:

> There is an even more compelling reason why the State should address the grievances of its employees: the concept of fair dealing between people. In the private sector, the government created the NLRA in an attempt to remove the coercive bargaining tactics used by employers in their pursuit of lucre. In so doing, it recognized the evils of a system based on the "take-it-or-leave it" philosophy of management-labor relations. As part of the remedy, certain rules were laid down which have the effect of balancing the parties' positions and encouraging a free exchange between management and labor. To say that the State is exempt from fair dealing is to allow the State to practice labor tactics as unfair as the type of tactics Congress outlawed under the NLRA. The State should be an example of highest order in regard to dealing fairly with workers.[76]

McGraw also specifically questioned the supposed public-private distinction as a basis upon which public employees could be reasonably treated in a disparate fashion, pointing out that, at that time in West Virginia, energy was managed privately, whereas the sale of alcohol was a state monopoly, and then asked rhetorically which function was properly deemed to be more essential for the public good.[77]

In 1979, staff at the municipally run Wetzel County Hospital requested that Local 1199 represent them in an organizing drive. The union sent organizer Danie Stewart, and in short order 80 percent of facility employees had signed authorization cards. A union proposal for negotiations was tersely rebuffed by hospital administration, citing the public facility's exemption from coverage under the National Labor Relations Board, setting the stage for a bitter eight-month struggle after repeated attempts to enter into discussions by the union.[78]

Once a strike had been called, the facility administration brought in union avoidance consultants and made moves to hire replacement workers to break the strike. A war over the hearts and minds of the community ensued, with the hospital organizing antiunion "concerned citizens" and hostile press coverage, and the union gaining community support and solidarity from the West Virginia Education Association and numerous private sector unions, as well as appealing to democratic, constitutional rights of freedom of speech, assembly, and association. One local newspaper countered the union's campaign by denouncing Stewart as a former member of Students for a Democratic Society, intent on overthrowing the government.[79]

The hospital did not relent and the organizing drive ended after the remaining strikers were fired on April 1, 1980. Fired employees, nevertheless, sought a measure of relief in circuit court with a civil suit exposing rampant corruption by hospital administrators that included bogus medical fees and theft of supplies by doctors who were also governing board members, along with practices of vendor bid-rigging and nepotism. The court eventually ordered the permanent removal of more than half of the governing board.[80]

Private Sector Postscript

Labor relations in the coal industry during the 1970s constituted a tumultuous background to what transpired in the public sector. As noted, one of Arnold Miller's first acts as UMWA president had been to support the Charleston city sanitation strike and publicly call for union rights for government employees. The decade, nevertheless, saw a drift by the new leadership of the UMWA away from its grassroots origins and an increasing distance from the rank and file of coal miners despite structural changes in union governance designed to institutionalize the demands for greater internal democracy.

Labor writer Cal Winslow describes the 1970s as a period in which frontline workers throughout the United States took up both the demand for participatory democracy that had been articulated in Students for a Democratic Society's "Port Huron Statement" and the demand for dignity that had defined the civil rights movement. As Winslow observes, "workers turned to direct action," and this turn finds its results in characterization of that period as a "strike wave."[81]

In West Virginia's coalfields, that grassroots militancy was repeatedly demonstrated by a continual surge in wildcat strikes. Nyden has noted that Miners for Democracy was quickly dismantled in the wake of the 1972 reform election victory, although the Black Lung Association continued as a vehicle for insurgency. Miller's alienation from the union membership was clearly evident in the negotiation of the 1974 industry-wide contract, and the "massive summer wildcats of 1975 and 1976." He found clear indications of the growing distrust of Miller's bureaucracy in the union's 1976 convention, when "delegates present literally wrote their proposed contract word-for-word on the convention floor, demanding foremost the right to strike during the term of the contract, which passed unanimously. A proposal by Miller's administration to institute disciplinary procedures against leaders of wildcats foundered when not a single delegate was willing to second."[82] The right-to-strike movement eventually succumbed to the bitter and grueling 110-day contract strike of 1977–78, during which the membership voted down a first proposal that "not only failed to contain the right to strike over unresolved local grievances, but gave management the right to fire or penalize anyone organizing, walking on, or honoring a picket line."[83] When miners rejected a second proposal, President Carter imposed a Taft-Hartley return to work order that was largely ignored by the strikers. Forced to give up many, though not all, concessions, the final offered version of March 24, 1978, was ratified by a slim margin with 65 percent of union members voting. Nyden's verdict was that the struggle failed because "no movement emerged from below to carry the union forward."[84]

Wildcat strikes, which were illegal in law and unsanctioned by the union bureaucracy, were, of course, a long tradition in the coalfields, predating the 1912–13 Cabin Creek–Paint Creek strike. Owing to the unwillingness of coal miners to cross picket lines, they were spread by the practice called "stranger" picketing, in which roving pickets from one mine would pull out workers at other mines.[85] This ethos of solidarity was cynically used by decidedly antiunion groups such as the Klan and the John Birch Society in an attempt to create an aura of populism during the 1974 Kanawha County textbook protests.[86] The right to strike movement during the 1970s was also seized upon by cadre of the Revolutionary Communist Party to give legitimacy to its Maoist ideology.[87] Treatments of the history of the party, interestingly, make little if any mention of its intervention in West Virginia's mine workers struggles.[88]

Although the 1970s proved to be a period of dramatic and continuous insurgency for the United Mine Workers of America, the history of labor relations in the private sector in West Virginia was drawing on a long-lasting tradition of industrial struggle that had only recently found an analogous expression for public workers. This accounts for why, in a law review article published in 1976, Charles Kincaid of the National Labor Relations Board was able to begin by citing Governor Moore's 1969 mass firing of striking state road workers, before observing: "It probably seems ironical that West Virginia, which is considered to have the most unionized private sector, has one of the least unionized state governments."[89]

CHAPTER 3

The 1980s

The 1980 Teachers' Strike

In March 21, 1980, thirty county affiliates of the West Virginia Education Association (WVEA) voted to walk out in protest of the state legislature's refusal to grant classroom instructors' request for a $3,000 pay increase, having passed a pay raise of $950 instead. Although eighteen of the remaining twenty-five counties voted not to join the strike, they nevertheless sent county delegations to a massive rally conducted in Charleston that same day.[1] As many as seven thousand rallied at an open-air sports stadium, undeterred by a torrential rainstorm, and the rally was followed by a march on the state capitol, which shut down traffic.[2]

The parent organization of the West Virginia Education Association, the National Education Association (NEA), has a history that is far from typical for what had become one of the nation's largest labor unions. When it was founded in 1857, NEA was a mostly male professional association of public-school administrators and superintendents. A separate internal department for classroom teachers did not exist in NEA until 1912 and a concerted effort to recruit teachers into NEA membership only began after the 1916 formation of the American Federation of Teachers (AFT) within the American Federation of Labor (AFL).[3]

In marked contrast to NEA, AFT was an avowed labor union from the outset, created by and for classroom teachers. Its locals were also predominately organized in cities, whereas NEA as a national organization was oriented toward rural areas. Marjorie Murphy writes that NEA began an organizational transformation from national departments when it began to emphasize state associations in the 1920s and then local chapters in the 1960s.[4] By restricting membership to classroom teachers, AFT was more leftist, and given the gender composition of teachers, more feminist for most of its existence. AFT promoted the goal of collective bargaining long before it was embraced by NEA, and perhaps more importantly, AFT locals were willing to strike, regardless of the universal illegality of that tactic in the public sector. And, until the rise of a more conservative leadership bureaucracy exemplified by Albert Shanker, AFT could contrast itself to NEA by a long history of alliance with the civil rights movement.[5] By 1980, however, when the West Virginia teachers' strike erupted, the same process noted by Murphy at a national level was reflected there as well. NEA and AFT had "nearly switched roles, with NEA taking bolder, more progressive positions on a range of social issues, while the union looks for creative yet conservative solutions to educational problem."[6]

The historical role-switching was not something that happened overnight in West Virginia, as was evidenced in the history of race relations among teachers. Beginning as an informal "reading circle" in Charleston, more than fifty Black teachers in West Virginia met in Charleston on November 27, 1891, to establish the West Virginia State Teachers Association (WVSTA).[7] WVEA and WVSTA soon initiated a practice of conducting their respective statewide meetings at the same time in the same city. According to Ancella Bickley, although neither group

> had constitutional provisions against membership by persons of the other race, there are no records of cross-racial memberships in the associations during the early years. Because Blacks had their own organization, they seldom applied for membership in WVEA. Had they applied, it is likely they would have been unsuccessful for the WVEA had a longstanding practice of refusing the acceptance of Blacks. There is no indication that Whites ever applied for membership in the black organization.[8]

Bickley observes that this segregation was somewhat eroded once the practice of payroll deductions for union dues began, making exclusion of Black teachers difficult, and in the early 1950s WVEA already had some county affiliates with racially mixed memberships. In 1954, the year of the momentous decision that struck down school segregation, *Brown v. Board of Education*, the formal merger of WVSTA with WVEA began.[9] The merger was not seamlessly smooth, however, and WVSTA was pressured to discontinue annual donations to the NAACP in order to placate WVEA objections.[10] Residual resistance to racial equality was evident when, in 1972, a Black caucus within WVEA was formed.[11]

By 1980, in West Virginia the state NEA affiliate was the largest public sector labor organization, each of the fifty-five county affiliates was the functional equivalent to a United Mine Workers of America (UMWA) local representing a particular mine, and county chapter members therefore would vote on whether or not to participate in the March 21 one-day walkout. While WVEA could recommend the action of a one-day walkout, it was the prerogative of each county association to decide whether to join or not. Given the illegality of any public worker strike, statements by participants at the time reflected a range of self-characterizations. The state school superintendent, under the administration of Governor Jay Rockefeller, attempted to head off the strike altogether by announcing schools would remain open and there would be no pay for striking teachers. The Hampshire County Education Association president informed the press that delegates attending the Charleston rally had been "properly excused" by the county board of education. The board of education in Kanawha County, aware that the Charleston rally was scheduled for one o'clock in the afternoon, announced that classes were dismissed after the morning session for "in-service teacher training." Despite a threat of discipline from far-right school board member Alice Moore, instigator of the 1974 textbook protest, Kanawha teachers took the entire day. Striking teachers in Kanawha and Jefferson counties announced that they would willingly forfeit a day's pay to attend.[12]

Although it was a limited one-day work stoppage and failed to extend beyond thirty counties, the 1980 teachers' strike demonstrated that the prospect of a public sector strike had not been permanently quelled by the draconian responses meted out to state road workers in 1969 and to Charleston city sanitation workers in 1972. As such it was a harbinger of progressively more extensive future struggles that were to emerge, particularly in West Virginia's public schools.

Historian William Hal Gorby has persuasively argued that the continuing reliance of state government in West Virginia on spending and taxation policies that were in conformity with neoliberalism beginning in the 1970s provides an explanatory context for the periodic eruption of protests about public education wages and working conditions. As evidence for that reliance, Gorby cites the prolonged legal dispute that resulted in what is generally known as the Recht Decision.[13] The West Virginia Supreme Court of Appeals remanded a late 1970s case challenging the constitutionality of the state's educational system and its financing mechanism to the Kanawha County Circuit Court.[14] As a result, on May 11, 1982, the Kanawha court issued a 244-page "Findings of Fact and Conclusions of Law, and Order" that mandated the development of a "Master Plan for Public Education," and approved a draft of that plan on March 4, 1983. After further litigation, the state's supreme court upheld the plan to bring school funding into alignment with the state's constitutional provisions for public education, and the duty of the West Virginia Board of Education "to determine educational policies of the State in conformity with constitutional and statutory mandates."[15] Gorby notes that it was in the aftermath of the educational funding controversy that Governor Arch Moore averted a threatened strike by WVEA in 1987 with the promise of a wage increase, and his failure to follow through with that promise only exacerbated an already contentious relation between public school teachers and state government.[16]

Local 1199 in 1980s West Virginia

In 1980, the year the state's higher court handed down the *City of Fairmont* decision, 1199's national union, NUHHCE, merged the West Virginia and Kentucky affiliates into a single district, which was further merged in 1982 with Local 1199's Ohio jurisdiction and designated as District 1199 WV/KY/OH. That same year, 1982, was when Local 1199 began signing up members among the employees of West Virginia's state-operated medical facilities, which included a variety of health institutions such as mental hospitals, nursing homes, and at least one general hospital, all of which—excepting state facilities devoted to military veterans—were eventually placed under the administration of the West Virginia Department of Health and Human Resources (DHHR), easily the largest of executive branch agencies and certainly the one benefiting the most from federal funding. By 1983, Local 1199 claimed to have a dues-paying membership of 1,100 in West Virginia's state facilities.[17]

Cabell Huntington Hospital was, as noted before, a public institution created by an act of the legislature in 1945, and its construction financed through bonds approved by the voters of Cabell County and City of Huntington. Its administration was statutorily vested in a board of trustees appointed by the county commission and its premises belonged jointly to the county and city. On April 16, 1984, administrators for Cabell Huntington announced their decision to lay off forty-three hospital employees, prompting Local 1199, which represented all but four of the positions slated for elimination, to publicly dispute the rationale of the impending layoffs.[18]

Beginning on May 9, 1984, Local 1199 began distributing leaflets at and around hospital premises contesting the firings and questioning management's decision to go forward. On May 11, 1984, in response to the leafleting, facility administrators issued a memorandum accusing Local 1199 of violating the existing contract by engaging in prohibited picketing of the facility prior to the expiration of the agreed contract. The next day, Cabell Huntington management fired nine workers for continuing to leaflet, and, on May 14, 1984, fired an additional five employees for further distribution of leaflets.

In contrast to the earlier action at Fairmont General, this time it was the union that went to court on May 14, 1984, and on May 15, 1984, in response to a writ of mandamus, the state's court issued a show cause order to Cabell Huntington based on the facility's summary dismissal of leafleting employees. The court would later note, "There is no indication that this distribution was anything but peaceful." The court, on May 30, 1984, ordered the hospital to reinstate the fired workers with back pay and would later determine that included among the leafleting employees, "were all of the local union officials and every hospital employee who was a union district official."[19]

The court also found that writ of mandamus was properly sought by the union: "By the terms of the collective bargaining agreement, the grievance and arbitration procedure contained therein is not the sole and exclusive avenue of relief in all disputes arising under the agreement, particularly with regard to grievances arising under the agreement's 'no strike' provision." Furthermore, the court found, "[The] primary issue presented in this action is whether the disciplinary actions taken by the hospital in response to the group distribution of leaflets by the fourteen hospital employees violated their free speech rights under the federal and state constitutions."[20]

In citing federal precedent for its ruling reversing Cabell Huntington's summary dismissal of leafleting workers in the union's favor, the state court held, "The United States Supreme Court has long held that public employees may not 'be compelled to relinquish the First Amendment rights they would otherwise enjoy as citizens to comment on matters of public interest in connection with the operation of the public [institutions] in which they work.'"[21]

The state court's own previous ruling was asserted in its decision: "Public employees are entitled to the protections afforded by the First and Fourteenth Amendments and any regulations pertaining to such employees must strike a balance between the interests of such an employee, as a citizen commenting on matters of public concern, and the interest of the state in promoting efficiency in its affairs."[22]

On July 11, 1984, in writing the opinion for *Woodruff v. Board of Trustees of Cabell Huntington Hospital*, Justice McGraw stated:

> In addition to the violation of the petitioner employees' fundamental constitutional rights under the state constitution, we also conclude that their termination violated their first amendment rights under the federal constitution. These inherent rights, of which members of society may not by contract divest themselves, include the freedoms of speech and press under article III, §7 of the West Virginia Constitution, and the rights to assemble, associate, and petition under article III, §16 of the West Virginia Constitution. No parallel provision to this section of our state constitution appears in the United States Constitution. Therefore, with respect to the waiver of fundamental constitutional rights, our state constitution is more stringent in its limitation on waiver than is the federal constitution.[23]

One of the less successful efforts of Local 1199 in West Virginia was in resisting ongoing attempts to close Spencer State Hospital, which at one point employed more than three hundred workers. In July, 1981, at a time when the state facility was celebrating eighty-eight years of operation, then-governor Jay Rockefeller had sought to quell community rumors that it was on the chopping block. Six months later, however, Rockefeller, citing a 10 percent state budget cut and the facility's failure to qualify for federal subsidies, announced the hospital's impending closure.[24]

Strong community and worker support for the facility's continuance included proposals to convert it into a psychiatric-geriatric facility, which would, it was assumed, qualify it for additional federal funding. In line with that scenario, the state legislature earmarked a portion of the state budget for Spencer Hospital, designating 1984 as the target date for federal certification.

Rockefeller refused to go along with the legislative measures to fund Spencer State Hospital's conversion, although a study indicated that the upgrade would be less costly than similar measures for psychiatric hospitals in both Huntington and Weston, and renovations could be completed in less than a year, enabling the facility to house 270 patients. The State Supreme Court of Appeals overturned the governor's budget veto, restoring nearly four million dollars to Spencer. Despite that, hospital administration subsequently laid off ninety-five employees.

Additional court rulings, arising from a decision known as *Hartley*, had mandated that the state move away from the institutionalization of mental patients toward a preference for treatment programs, a transition that was meant to begin in 1983 and would include lessening reliance on confinement and sedation of psychiatric patients. In 1984 and 1985, however, hospital staff injuries began to soar, and a union survey found that Spencer State Hospital, due to chronic understaffing, suffered the highest injury rate of any state facility, with more than 1,400 in a five-month period in 1985.

Arch Moore began a new term as governor in 1985, replacing Rockefeller. While his proposed state budget initially dedicated funds for Spencer State Hospital's conversion to a new facility, with federal certification scheduled for 1989, Moore subsequently imposed a severe budget reduction and laid off additional hospital staff. Interestingly, Moore attended a groundbreaking ceremony at the Spencer site for a new facility in 1988, which went no further than architectural plans.

The *Hartley* decision, premised on deinstitutionalization of psychiatric patients and the creation of community group home settings, went unrealized by the state. Nevertheless, adequate funding and staffing of existing facilities such as Spencer State Hospital continued to go unrealized as well.

Statehouse political operators played the issue both ways by citing fiscal obstacles to adequate staffing of the facility, and fomenting community fears about the presence of violent psychiatric patients should any solutions mandated under the *Hartley* decision be implemented. Facility patients and employees were both caught between the jaws of a political vise, and in June of 1989, Spencer State Hospital was closed permanently.

The precarity of West Virginia's state health facilities and the implications of that precarity for its residents, patients, employees, and home communities, as well as the implications of *Hartley*, would continue to reverberate long after Local 1199's decision to completely abandon the union's state hospital membership two decades later. At any rate, 1989 would also be the year that 1199's national union made the decision to merge with the Service Employees International Union (SEIU) and its West Virginia, Kentucky, and Ohio district became SEIU District 1199/WV/KY/OH. The extent to which the merger with SEIU would limit 1199's continued involvement in West Virginia's public sector struggles may be speculative, but it is difficult to entirely dismiss a presumption that 1199's absorption into one of the largest national unions contributed to a diminished emphasis on organizing the workforces of the numerous state-run health facilities.[25]

Testing the Waters for Collective Bargaining

Unlike Virginia and North Carolina, West Virginia remained in a legal limbo: public sector collective bargaining was not specifically prohibited, nor was it specifically mandated. As such, the unions that were pushing for a bargaining regime comparable to that of the private sector under the auspices of the National Labor Relations Board were left to continually play out organizing struggles in the courts.

On February 25, 1982, the City of Huntington, a longtime labor stronghold in terms of private industry, entered into a one-year, seventeen-page written contract with three hundred city sanitation workers in AFSCME Local 598 that covered wages, leave time, seniority, a grievance procedure, and additional matters. One provision of the "employment agreement" required parity with other city workers, specifically, that sanitation workers would receive raises whenever other organized municipal departments such as fire and police received pay increases.[26]

When the city's administration sought to violate the parity compensation provision, the case made its way to the state supreme court, with AFSCME gaining legal support from both WVEA and UMWA. The position adopted by the City of Huntington was that there was no binding legal basis requiring the municipality to honor labor contracts into which it had voluntarily entered, that doing so was outside the scope of their power. Huntington cited as support for this argument a February 23, 1966, opinion of the state's attorney general which held, "The final determination of wages, hours, working conditions and the like, rests with the particular governmental unit and cannot be delegated away."[27]

On June 13, 1984, Justice Richard Neely, writing for the court, found that any public body that enters into a collectively bargained agreement is not improperly delegating away its governing authority. Furthermore, the court agreed with AFSCME Local 598 that the "failure of the legislature to enact a particular law is not evidence that the legislature rejected the policy underlying collective bargaining." The decision further noted that Huntington had a ten-year history of entering into collective bargaining agreements such as the one for sanitation employees, which include no-strike, no-lockout provisions, and could not hold those employees to those terms if it was unwilling to honor the negotiated agreement itself.[28]

The enforceability of collective bargaining contracts with public sector entities was again considered by the courts in 1987. Central West Virginia Transit Authority had entered into an agreement on July 1, 1981, that established a grievance procedure as well as containing a clause allowing unresolved grievances to be appealed to arbitration. After a November 19, 1982, grievance had been filed by the union, Local Division 812 of the Amalgamated Transit Union (ATU), which contested a November 12, 1982, discharge from employment of a driver, the employer upheld the dismissal on November 26, 1982. Soon after, the union notified the employer that it was appealing the matter directly to arbitration.[29]

The Transit Authority refused to proceed to arbitration by citing what it designated as procedural errors, i.e., improperly going to arbitration after the first step and being untimely in any appeal to the second step. Once the matter had entered into formal litigation, the Transit Authority additionally asserted that, as an unincorporated entity, the local had no standing to bring legal action before the court.[30]

Justice Thomas McHugh, writing for the State Supreme Court of Appeals, ruled that there existed in legal precedence a presumption in favor of the recourse to arbitration in employment matters, that the exercise of such a recourse was consistent with the bargaining agreement between ATU and the Transit Authority, that the union had legal standing to bring action, and, importantly in the instant case, disputes regarding procedural issues were themselves matters properly to be addressed in the arbitration process.[31]

Legal Changes for State Employees

In the early 1980s, legislative statutory allowance for union membership dues to be deducted from the paychecks of state employees set off an uptick in organizing efforts by some AFL-affiliated unions, along with the potential for competition and even raiding of each other, although generally they were willing to draw jurisdictional boundaries between various agencies and to concentrate organizing drives to mutually recognized targets.[32]

Local 1199, now renamed District 1199, was content to limit its state worker recruitment to various health facilities such as the long-term care nursing homes and psychiatric hospitals or health clinics operated by the state, with each state facility granted a chapter status. In 1983, AFSCME created Organizing Council 996 to encompass both state employees as well as city and county workers. The Communications Workers of America (CWA) founded Local 2055 in 1984 as a statewide organization specifically for corrections employees. The Laborers' International Union of North America established Local 814 for nonteaching personnel at West Virginia University and began bargaining for "memoranda of accord" even before the legislative adoption of dues checkoffs.

The early twentieth-century rival of the AFL, the syndicalist-oriented Industrial Workers of the World (IWW), criticized the AFL not only for its craft union orientation and its business unionist model but also for the separation between affiliates, preferring instead "one big union" to unite the entire working class organizationally. Although, or perhaps because, the various AFL components expressed a common interest in achieving the goal of collective bargaining, overcoming the "American fragmentation of labor" proved problematic in practice.[33] In the absence of a recognized exclusive representation afforded by prevailing American models of collective bargaining, a potential for friction between rival unions continued throughout the decade following the codification of union dues checkoffs.

Five years after the WVEA walkout, the state legislature created the West Virginia Education Employees Grievance Board, which covered public school employees as well as higher education employees at the state's colleges and universities, and during its existence issued roughly five hundred decisions. On July 1, 1988, with the addition of grievance jurisdiction to all state employees, the agency was renamed the West Virginia Education and State Employees Grievance Board. The agency was overseen by a board composed of three persons appointed by the governor and staffed by administrative law judges. Codification of an employee grievance procedure is a standard part of negotiated contracts. Repeated attempts by the state federation of the AFL-CIO to lobby on behalf of public employee collective bargaining provisions—in what was perhaps the state with the highest density of union membership during that period, and however much the state legislature was controlled by the Democratic Party—were met with failure.[34] In its initial incarnation, the grievance procedure was a four-step process, only the last step of which was a board decision, appealable to county circuit court.[35]If the enactment of a grievance procedure was a measure meant to placate any demand for full-blown unionization of the state's public sector workers, administrative agencies nevertheless from the outset sought to restrict the legislative granting of grievance rights. The state Health Department—forerunner of what would become, until its dissolution in 2023, the Department of Health and Human Resources—sought to impose a requirement that all third level hearings be conducted at the agency's administrative offices in Charleston. Since the agency included facilities and offices scattered around the state, such as the psychiatric Weston State Hospital and Welch Emergency Hospital in McDowell County, this presented a logistical inconvenience for both grieving employees and any witnesses they sought to call at hearing. The agency compounded this with refusals to allow employees use of office equipment and copies of level three transcripts for the preparation of appeals.[36]

District 1199 challenged the state health agency's obstruction of employee use of the grievance procedure by a writ of mandamus. Justice William Brotherton wrote the West Virginia Supreme Court of Appeal's decision granting relief to the union based on the clear wording of the 1988 statute, "We, therefore, conclude that the employer has a duty to hold the hearing at the worksite unless otherwise agreed to by the parties. We also find that the aggrieved employee has the right to use, free of charge, the employer's copy machine for the purpose of copying grievance documents and the transcript of the employment grievance hearing."[37]

Perhaps more significant for existing labor unions during the 1980s was the establishment of a state employee union dues checkoff. Again, this was simply the adoption of a practice that had not been previously prohibited under law. As early as August 29, 1975, the state's attorney general issued an opinion that it was permissible for a state employee to agree to have union dues deducted from their wages and for "each spending unit of state government to amend its payroll procedures to permit such deductions to be made."[38]

Precarity of the Grievance Procedure

The imposition of a dress code on public employees might strike some observers as a trivial issue with regard to the continual contest between state authority and public employees, at most a residual matter from the 1960s counterculture.[39] The West Virginia Public Employees Association had raised the matter in the 1970s when a state agency had unilaterally imposed an outdated, arbitrary and restrictive dress code that had no perceptible relevance to the effective provision of services to the public. It would continue to be a notably frequent arena of contestation between state power and public workers well into the twenty-first century, reminiscent of debates about whether public service employees were "professionals" rather than "workers," and the variant implications of those designations on the propriety of unionization.

A flurry of grievances at the end of the 1980s, all involving a classroom teacher, illustrated the ways in which that matter could implicate any number of issues effecting the legal status of public employees. On August 29, 1988, the newly appointed Mason County superintendent of schools distributed guidelines for mandated attire for the impending 1988–89 school year that prohibited "professional employees" from wearing jeans and, if the teacher was male, required them to wear ties, citing a statement of the state schools superintendent as warrant for imposing those restrictions. That policy was, moreover, implemented without any prior formal consideration or adoption by the school board and without any consultation with the effected staff.[40]

William Webb, a popular, twenty-year tenured teacher with no previous performance issues was suspended twice in quick succession, on September 16 and September 27, 1988, for refusal to comply with the code. Webb filed grievance on grounds that the requirement was outside the terms of his continuing contract of employment and that the superintendent had imposed the policy without prior school board approval. The rationale for a dress code offered by the superintendent was that such a policy would instill a sense "of order and discipline" in students and that Webb was "setting a bad example ... by continuing to defy authority." After the state grievance board denied Webb's grievance, he appealed to circuit court in Kanawha County, and in June 7, 1989, the denial was reversed on grounds that the dress code had not been adopted by the school board when the suspensions were imposed.[41]

However, during the period in which the suspension was moving through litigation, the Mason County Board of Education adopted a modified version of the dress code that retained the ban on teachers wearing denim jeans on November 21, 1988. On December 21, 1988, Webb was dismissed from employment for gross insubordination, and he again filed a grievance. As part of his defense, Webb cited constitutional grounds for academic freedom and freedom of expression, as well as the lack of mention for an instructional dress code in state public school law, despite provisions for uniforms for service personnel. The latter argument involved the claim that the school board lacked statutory authority to regulate instructional attire. The grievance board again denied his grievance, and that denial was also reversed by the circuit court.[42]

In the midst of all of this litigation, on November 24, 1988, the school district presented Webb with an invoice for his daughter's out-of-state education since he resided across the state line in Ohio. His daughter had attended school in Mason County for several years, and in return Webb had continually taught extra classes for no pay. Webb filed a third grievance charging illegal retaliation for his having previously filed grievance, and this time the grievance board granted his claim.[43]

CHAPTER 4

The 1990s

The 1990 Teachers' Strike

On March 7, 1990, public school teachers in forty-seven of the state's fifty-five counties set up picket lines, beginning a strike that was more extensive geographically and longer lasting than the single-day 1980 walkout. The strike came on the heels of a ten-month United Mine Workers of America (UMWA) strike against Pittston Coal that had been marked by clashes between workers and the company, including the sit-in occupation of a processing plant and other instances of civil disobedience. The success of the Pittston strike in shoring up the miners' retirement would certainly have resonated with teachers who faced not only the perennial issue of low pay but also shortfalls in legislative funding for their health coverage under the Public Employees Insurance Agency (PEIA).[1] The PEIA was founded in 1972 as the Public Employees Insurance Board to provide health insurance for state workers and public education workers, including teachers. Throughout its history, PEIA has been a chimera agency resembling in part a state program and in part a shifting experiment in privatization. It has remained for almost the entirety of its existence an exercise in fiscal austerity, chronically underfunded by the legislature with steadily increasing cost-shifting to public workers in lieu of state budgetary provision of adequate appropriations. When it was renamed as PEIA in 1988, a modest infusion of money was offset by the imposition of deductibles and fees, and PEIA became a flashpoint—not for the last time—for the 1990 teacher strike.[2]

As noted by historian William Hal Gorby, there had been loud rumblings of teacher dissatisfaction with the deterioration of wages and health benefits throughout the 1980s.[3] Gaston Caperton had become governor in 1988 and had enjoyed an early endorsement from the West Virginia Education Association (WVEA), which helped to overcome his lack of previous political experience and clout, but the union's initial expectations of receptiveness from the newly elected governor were disappointed. Two years into the Caperton administration, patience among educators had run thin with the governor's acquiescence to political pressures for fiscal austerity after having campaigned on promises to address low teacher pay.[4] Caperton announced during the 1990 legislative session that there would be no raises, and in light of that reversal coupled with previous cuts in health insurance, a number of WVEA affiliates, particularly in the southern coalfield counties, began conducting strike authorization votes in February, defying the plan of state union leadership to wait until May to take action.[5]

On February 15, 1990, six thousand teachers, most of them WVEA members, rallied at the state capitol, demanding pay raises and funding for PEIA, and disrupting the legislative business. On March 5, state politicians met with WVEA and American Federation of Teachers–West Virginia (AFT-WV) leaders to work out a deal. While, as in 1980, WVEA members played a leading role in starting the strike, the other teacher labor organization, the AFT–WV, had grown in membership in the previous decade, making that union's participation of some importance to conducting any strike.[6] By this time, however, the relative militancy of the two teacher unions had undergone a reversal of the roles they had played decades before.[7] Whereas Bob Brown, AFT-WV's director, urged acceptance of the negotiated compromise, WVEA's elected president, Kayetta Meadows, openly expressed reservations about accepting a no-strike provision that had been demanded by political officials as a precondition to a final agreement.[8] If the political powers-that-be believed the strike talk was an empty threat, or that the union leaders could rein in the membership, they miscalculated. County by county, teachers began walking off the job beginning on March 6. Caught off guard, state administrators threatened injunctions and job discipline for strikers, and sought to prevent picketing.[9]

The use of picket lines in the 1990 teacher strike took on an added significance in light of the need to obstruct the operation of school buses to close down schools effectively. Because the union that represented school bus drivers, the West Virginia School Service Personnel Association (WVSSPA), had withheld support for the strike, picketing the entrances of bus garages became a feature of the contentious walkout.[10] Seven striking teachers in Kanawha County were arrested for using vehicles to block the entrance to a county bus garage.[11]

On March 8, 1990, the state's attorney general issued an opinion at the request of the state superintendent of schools that "no right to strike against the state" existed. The opinion relied on an extensive restatement of the federal court ruling in *Kirker v. Moore.*[12] On March 12, 1990, the Jefferson County Board of Education secured a preliminary injunction in county circuit court against striking members of WVEA declaring that the strike was illegal. On April 12, 1990, the state supreme court ruled that in the absence of enabling state legislation, common law warranted agreement that "public employees do not have the right to strike." The court additionally cited federal rulings, including *Kirker v. Moore* and *United Federation of Postal Clerks v. Blount* (1971). The decision went on to conclude that neither the *City of Fairmont* nor *Woodruff* decision involving Cabell Huntington Hospital supported the right of WVEA members to strike.[13]

Despite AFT-WV being a listed party in the supreme court case, WVEA was the major teacher organization at the time with an estimated statewide membership of 16,000 teachers out of a total teaching workforce of 22,000, and WVEA members played the most significant role throughout the work stoppage. The strike itself, however, did not end until March 17, when a settlement was reached with the legislators negotiating with the teacher organizations. The agreement provided for pay increases along with promises to develop plans for strengthening educational resources as well as an August special legislative session to be focused on education. In a survey of public sector employee organizations conducted soon after, it was observed that if teachers had been inspired in 1990 by the mineworkers in the immediate years preceding their walkout, the example of the teachers might, in turn, reverberate with other public workers.[14]

West Virginia Public Employees Union

In 1991 and 1992, Phil Edwards conducted a series of surveys of public employee organizations in West Virginia. Eleven unions and employee associations having state and/or local public worker memberships submitted responses to a questionnaire that covered areas of organizing, institutional experience with the state grievance procedure, stance toward collective bargaining, and a range of related issues and concerns. The survey was conducted under the auspices of the Southern West Virginia Center for Labor Management Initiatives and was the brainchild of that organization's coordinator, the noted West Virginia labor historian Frederick Barkey. A draft of the survey results, *Status Report on Public Employee Organizations in West Virginia,* provided the only comprehensive inquiry undertaken to date into the history of public worker unions in what has been, historically, the most unionized southern state.

Only two organizations at that time declared an opposition to public employee collective bargaining: the independent WVSSPA, with more than eleven thousand members, and the antiunion West Virginia Professional Educators (WVPE), with around four hundred. Of the employee organizations subject to the state grievance board, only the WVPE took the position that the statutory grievance procedure was, in its implementation, fair and not partial to the employer. WVPE in other respects responded to the survey as one would expect from a "company union," explicit in its condemnation of the WVEA-led 1990 strike.

The greatest anomaly noted in the status report was the low rate of public sector unionization in West Virginia. Edwards recorded, as a possible countervailing factor, the 1991 formation of the West Virginia State Employees Union (WVSEU) as a joint venture of the American Federation of State, County and Municipal Employees (AFSCME), Communication Workers of America (CWA),

Service Employees International Union (SEIU), and UMWA. Those AFL-CIO affiliates, under the auspices of WVSEU, unsuccessfully "conducted an aggressive campaign for the legalization of public employee collective bargaining during the 1992 legislative session," that nevertheless resulted in Governor Caperton convening a "blue ribbon" commission to "study the question."[15]

In Edwards's description of WVSEU as a new union that "merged" the public worker branches of existing AFL-CIO unions, it was clearly regarded by him as potential corrective to the long-existing absence of cooperation among public employee organizations, which Edwards saw as a factor obstructing the achievement of public sector collective bargaining in West Virginia. Nevertheless, it appears that AFSCME Organizing Council 996, Local 7777, tended to dominate the new formation throughout its brief history. It is worth noting that the documentary collection for WVSEU for the years 1991–95, housed and archived at the Walter P. Reuther Library of Wayne State University, was donated by AFSCME.

A writ of mandamus filed by WVSEU before the West Virginia Supreme Court of Appeals on February 8, 1994, originated within the AFSCME jurisdictional agencies of the State Road Commission, by then designated as the Division of Highways, and the Department of Health and Human Resources, the two largest executive state agencies. That case involved a statewide reclassification plan by the Division of Personnel which had already been implemented on November 21, 1991, within a series of smaller agencies without having first conducted a public hearing. When the plan was extended to the Division of Highways and Department of Health and Human Resources in December 1992, WVSEU sought the writ, which was denied because of the union's lateness in making the complaint.

In the summer of 1996, AFSCME spearheaded an organizing blitz of state workers, recruiting more than eight hundred new members for WVSEU. It is telling that, at that time, WVSEU's president was an AFSCME highway worker, Jerry Lilly, and the director for WVSEU was Dave Bielski, who was also an AFSCME regional director. In July 1997, AFSCME Local 7777 was dissolved and in its place was created AFSCME/West Virginia State Employees Union (WVSEU) Council 77, which encompassed all West Virginia AFSCME members, state as well as municipal. The first president of Council 77 was Rod Riggleman, president of AFSCME Local 743, composed of City of Clarksburg Sanitary Board employees. The experiment of an interorganizational state worker union in order to achieve public employee collective bargaining was at an evident end.

The death knell for WVSEU was quite likely to be found in the November 5, 1996, defeat of the Democratic nominee for governor Charlotte Pritt. WVSEU had campaigned energetically on behalf of Pritt, who had promised implementation of an executive order creating public employee collective bargaining which, after years of failing to get enacted through the state legislature, seemed to be the last best hope of realizing that prospect.[16]

Charlotte Pritt Campaign

In 1996, Charlotte Pritt, a legislative delegate perhaps best known for the successful expansion of parental medical leave for employees as a supplement to the federal Family Medical Leave Act, sought the nomination for Democratic Party candidate for governor. It was not her first try. In 1992, in the wake of the massive teachers strike, she had vied with political newcomer and insurance executive Gaston Caperton for the gubernatorial nomination in a three-way race where she was bested by Caperton after he had spent ten times as much as her in the campaign. Pritt based much of her criticism of Caperton during the primary on his opposition to public employee collective bargaining as well as his support for regressive taxation in the form of grocery and gasoline taxes.

By 1996, however, Pritt, supported by the teacher unions and the UMWA, defeated her challenger for the nomination, Joe Manchin, a probusiness, antilabor conservative. The state's corporate elite—including much of the Democratic Party establishment led by Manchin—were alarmed by the prospect of a prolabor governor, and rallied around the resurrected figure of former governor Cecil Underwood, who had secured the Republican nomination.

West Virginia's Democratic Party had remained electorally successful long after other southern states had transitioned first to Dixiecrats and then Republicans in political dominance. This was doubtlessly due to the ability of probusiness elements, particularly the coal industry, to exercise clout within the state's Democratic Party.

Pritt's defeat in the general election of 1996 can be seen as the last chapter in the long-running feud between New Deal and corporatist factions in the Democratic Party. That feud was evident, for example, when William Casey Marland, a New Deal Democrat, had been narrowly elected governor in 1952. During his administration, Marland had helped defuse the Dixiecrat fate that had swept other southern states when he implemented public school desegregation in the wake of *Brown v. Board of Education* (1954). However, when Marland had the temerity to propose a severance tax on coal production in order to shore up the state's fiscal health and fund educational and social welfare development, the party's conservative faction, which was nominally in control of the state's party organization as well as the legislature, went after Marland in a concerted campaign of marginalization and vilification, a factor that ultimately fed into the end of his political prospects.[17]

The demise of Pritt's bid for governor also supports a contention that West Virginia's Democratic Party had become more often than not aligned with the neoliberal agenda that shaped the state's public policies during that party's long dominance of the legislature, as well as during the Rockefeller and Caperton administrations.[18] That contention is also supported by the repeated unwillingness of successive Democratic Party governors and decades of Democratic domination of the legislature to bring about public employee collective bargaining. An unwavering adherence to neoliberal policy would also define the long career of Pritt's chief political nemesis, Joe Manchin.

Laborers Local 814

Conflict between unions seeking to organize West Virginia's public sector workplaces was not confined to the WVEA and AFT-WV rivalry over public school teachers. On May 25, 1990, the state grievance board received an appeal on behalf of the University Association of Concerned Employees, affiliated with AFSCME District 996, seeking recognition and bargaining rights through a memorandum of accord with West Virginia University. The AFSCME grievance specifically charged that the university had demonstrated discrimination by means of a long-standing memorandum of accord with Local 814 of the Laborers' International Union of North America (LIUNA) that granted the latter union exclusive official recognition and other provisions, including monthly meetings between Local 814 and college administrators sometimes known as "meet-and-confer." AFSCME's requested relief was to either be granted a similar memorandum of accord or to hold what amounted to a certification election within the bargaining units to determine which union would gain recognition.[19]

The memorandum of accord with Local 814 had existed since the late 1960s, was renegotiated in 1982, and in 1991 reportedly covered 350 nonclerical support staff employed by the university.[20] As such, the relationship between the Laborers' International Union and West Virginia University was a sort of hybrid arrangement of union recognition. Local 814, however, included within its membership a collection of both public and nonprofit workplaces, the latter being, as private employers, covered under the law permitting full-blown collective bargaining. For example, Local 814 had first achieved union recognition for custodial, grounds, and maintenance workers at West Virginia Wesleyan College in Buckhannon on June 13, 1977, and was regularly able to negotiate contracts for those members. A similar unit of service and maintenance employees was covered by the local at Jackson General Hospital.

The continuing representation at West Virginia University had been further complicated when, in 1984, West Virginia University Hospital was severed from the university as a private, nonprofit entity.[21] The privatization of West Virginia University Hospital from the parent institution was at the time only the second such divestment in the US, and decades later, West Virginia University Medicine would become the single largest employer in the state.[22]

One of the consequences of the privatization of the medical facility was that, while West Virginia University employees continued under the existing memorandum of accord, those who became West Virginia University Hospital employees could be covered under a collectively bargained contract with Local 814. However, one of the provisions in the enabling legislation was that hospital employees could retain the right to remain public employees with civil service protections rather than choose to become employees of the legally distinct new private entity of West Virginia University Hospital.[23] Because there were differing hospital employee seniority provisions for Local 814 members who remained under the memorandum of accord and those members who opted to be regarded as private personnel at the hospital, this led to some ambiguity when internal job selection issues arose. Thus, in 1993, a public employee board grievance judge concluded that although "the hiring process that was followed was far from ideal," there was no legal basis to apply memorandum of accord seniority requirements to a hospital employee who had nevertheless elected to remain a public employee after privatization.[24]

Public Sector Litigation

At least among the public worker union officials surveyed in the 1992 *Status Report,* there was little to no confidence expressed regarding the fairness of the public employee grievance procedure, a judgment confirmed in the grievance board's own annual reports, which indicated that that, for the length of its existence, final grievance decisions granted in favor of the employee has been fewer than 15 percent. That being said, there were some cases in the 1990s that had long-term impact on the working conditions of public workers that merit attention.

One initial controversy that arose had to do with the extent of the board's jurisdiction, as well as with legislatively created civil service protections. In an early case, *Seddon v. Kanawha-Charleston Health Department,* a county employee contested whether her dismissal was based upon good cause. Even before a determination in that question could be rendered, it was initially incumbent upon the board to decide whether or not the grievance procedure was available to an employee of a county health department.[25] An initial finding was made that the county health department was, in fact, a public agency created by legislation that fell within the meaning of the state employee grievance procedure. In addition to citing legislation, the board decision also cited an April 18, 1990, opinion of the state's attorney general that concluded that local county boards of health had adopted the state civil service system, and were compelled to follow the personnel policies that applied to classified service.

It was further concluded in *Seddon* that the employer's allegations upon which the grievant, a long-term employee in the classified service, was fired were based solely upon hearsay, which was deemed to be evidence insufficient to meet the burden of proof—a preponderance of the evidence—required in order to establish good cause in the dismissal of a civil service employee. As a consequence, the employer was ordered to restore the worker to employment with back pay and benefits.

Seddon, however, was overruled in a grievance filed shortly after a nurse employed by the Boone County Health Department alleged job misclassification. In that case, the grievance board accepted the agency's argument that the board lacked jurisdiction to hear and decide the disputed matter. This was affirmed on an appeal to the Boone County Circuit Court on November 24, 1993.[26] On appeal to the state supreme court, however, the question of jurisdiction in the public employee grievance decision was reversed and the case remanded, under reasoning that was similar to the argument that had been used earlier to decide *Seddon*.[27]

The status of unions within the public workplace also became an issue in grievance procedures during the decade. In one lengthy and complex decision in 1991, *Graley v. West Virginia Parkways Economic Development and Tourism Authority*, an at-will employee of the state's parkways authority alleged that his dismissal was wrongful and had been in retaliation for his union membership and activity in AFSCME. The board in *Graley* determined that the existence of an agency personnel handbook gave rise to an implied contract of employment, which created an exception to the ability to fire an at-will employee without good cause. It was further found that the constitutional freedom to affiliate with a union was a substantial public policy that constituted an additional exception to the ability to fire an employee without cause. Finally, the board found that the employee must prevail in an allegation of illegal retaliation if the agency could not rebut its having occurred.[28]

In addition to public employee grievance decisions, the rights of public workers were additionally adjudicated during this period in cases before state courts. One heretofore unprecedented issue arose after the Mid-Ohio Valley Transit Authority (MOVTA) was created as a public corporation, and on July 8, 1990, employees seeking collective bargaining rights with the representation of the United Steelworkers of America were denied recognition by MOVTA. On August 24, 1990, those employees filed a complaint in Wood County Circuit Court seeking an order for the transit authority to grant the union recognition and bargain with the union for a contract. Upon the ruling denying the complaint, the union appealed to the state supreme court, and cited *West Virginia Code* §8-27-21—the West Virginia Urban Mass Transportation Authority Act—which provided that when any public authority acquired an existing system, collective bargaining rights "shall be continued with respect to employees of any acquired system."[29]

Justice Workman, writing for the majority, concluded that the correct interpretation of the statute was that a collective bargaining agreement must have already been in place before MOVTA assumed control of the operation of the mass transit system, irrespective of whether the effected employees were already existing employees that were endowed with collective bargaining rights. Citing *City of Fairmont,* Justice Workman asserted that public employers may not be compelled to recognize a union. In his dissent, Chief Justice McHugh pointed out that the majority had misplaced the term "existing" to illiberally infer that the legislation required an existing collective bargaining agreement, as opposed to the existence of collective bargaining rights.[30]

Nevertheless, the restrictive reading rendered in *Kirkpatrick* was to later to receive a permissive application with far-reaching implications for public employee bargaining rights. On June 8, 1971, Amalgamated Transit Union (ATU) Local 1539 was granted recognition as the bargaining agent for the transportation department comprising bus operators, mechanics, and maintenance personnel of the Logan County Board of Education. Subsequently, Logan County and ATU Local 1539 negotiated contracts in 1971, 1980, and 1981. A provision of the 1981 contract stated, "[The contract] shall remain in effect for an indefinite period, or until such time as either party desires to initiate changes. At such time, the party which desires changes shall notify the other party at least ninety (90) days in advance."[31]

A grievance was filed by the thirty-one members of the local when, in May 2001, the board of education asserted that it was no longer under any obligation to recognize ATU Local 1539. The grievance decision ordering Logan County to recognize and bargain with the union cited *City of Huntington* that "notwithstanding the absence of a statutory provision authorizing public employee bargaining, a municipality or governmental entity may voluntarily enter into a collective bargaining agreement." Citing *Kirkpatrick*, the grievance decision concluded that the Logan County school board was "obligated to continue this relationship unless and until it properly notifies the Union it wishes to alter the terms or terminate the contract."[32]

The education sector unions had historically lobbied the state legislature for pay improvements, as well as increased funding and better terms for health insurance and retirement benefits. Legislators proved more amenable to changes in working conditions that could be made in lieu of those that entailed fiscal considerations, including those that had to do with statutory language governing the right to seniority protections in matters of promotion and filling vacant positions. The union representing school service personnel had achieved important seniority provisions since 1981, but WVEA was also able to get somewhat more favorable state code on seniority for teachers as well.[33]

In 1983, state code affecting teachers was amended to require seniority to have "a bearing on the selection process when applicants have otherwise equivalent qualifications or where the differences in qualification criteria are insufficient to form the basis for an informed and rational decision."[34] Teachers who resign and later seek to be rehired should not be disadvantaged just because it would be more cost effective to hire less experienced teachers.[35] Eventually, the state supreme court ruled that hiring decisions should be based on qualifications that include past service, but that it was only "when all other factors are equal should a board of education look to seniority."[36]

With this background of shifting application of teacher seniority, a case arose when a long-time tenured instructor resigned and later returned to work as a substitute teacher. After numerous unsuccessful applications for full-time employment, she filed a grievance contesting her repeated nonselection for available vacancies alleging, among other things, that her past experience, which should have granted her a measure of seniority, was improperly discounted by the school administration in favor of less experienced applicants. The grievance board ultimately ruled on the school board's behalf, denying her grievance.[37] After an unsuccessful appeal to county court, the matter went before the state supreme court in a case styled as *Triggs v. Berkeley County Board of Education*. Despite the dissent of Chief Justice McHugh, the court's majority concluded that there was no restoration of seniority after a teacher had resigned.[38]

The establishment of faculty senates in public schools had been one of the employee gains that resulted from the 1990 teacher strike. When the faculty senate of Danville Grade School sought to discuss collective bargaining at its meeting on November 6, 1992, the school principal prohibited the inclusion of the topic in the meeting agenda, a decision that was challenged in a grievance by teachers in attendance. The state grievance board would ultimately rule in favor of the county administration, citing *Board of Education v. Education Association* and concluding that the legislation establishing faculty senates did not extend to even allowing a discussion of collective bargaining.[39]

The generally antilabor tenor of the courts during the 1990s was also manifested in a ruling from the state supreme court holding that the civil service provisions supporting pay equity, as amended in 1993, did not prevent agencies from disregarding matters of equal pay and seniority by allowing "the state to pay employees within the same classification differing amounts."[40]

CHAPTER 5

The 2000s

American Federation of State, County and Municipal Employees, Council 77

On March 26, 2001, the American Federation of State, County and Municipal Employees (AFSCME) chartered Local 3248 to include state employees of Kanawha, Putnam, Boone, and Clay counties, excluding, however, workers in those counties who were already members of two existing locals, one drawn from the state's Division of Highways (DOH) and one for the Parkways Authority, both being agencies under the West Virginia Department of Transportation. The jurisdiction for the local included the seat of state government and the state capitol complex, thereby potentially taking in a considerable number of state employees.[1] Executive branch state agencies were required by law to have their principal headquarters within Charleston, so that—apart from local agency branch offices maintained throughout the state, or various state hospitals, nursing homes, correctional facilities, colleges, and universities—a state worker most likely worked from an office in the state capitol.

Because of an arrangement established within the state federation of the AFL-CIO after the demise of the West Virginia State Employees Union (WVSEU), employees of specific agencies were separately divvied up by AFSCME, Communications Workers of America (CWA), Service Employees International Union (SEIU), and United Mine Workers of America (UMWA), an arrangement that had preceded the formation of the WVSEU. The CWA laid claim to the prisons and state police. SEIU reasserted its traditional hold in state health facilities. The miners' union grabbed a handful of assorted small agencies including General Services and the Office of Miners Health, Safety and Training. The American Federation of Teachers (AFT), at least in theory, regarded higher education facilities as its allotted turf. The remaining clusters of state workers, a clear majority, were assigned to AFSCME. In the absence of public employment bargaining agreements, union membership remained strictly voluntary, and union density among state agencies remained low, despite West Virginia's reputation as the most unionized of southern states.[2]

According to Mary Ann Uzelac, a Department of Health and Human Resources (DHHR) employee during that time, AFSCME's state affiliate had gone through six executive directors in rapid succession by 2001, a fact she took as an indication of organizational instability.[3] Uzelac had previously been a union staff employee for AFSCME, WVSEU, and UMWA, as well as a field examiner for the National Labor Relations Board (NLRB), and her experiences with and criticisms of AFSCME in West Virginia were not limited to her observation concerning turnover in the executive director position of Council 77.[4] She attributed much of the blame for AFSCME's failure to organize West Virginia's state employees to the state federation of the AFL-CIO, specifically for what she described as its tepid support for public sector collective bargaining. That was compounded, in Uzelac's analysis, with the internecine warfare between the teacher's unions, which she also faulted for a residual mentality of professionalism. By way of a resolution, Uzelac announced the founding of the Independent Union of Public Employees.[5]

Although Uzelac expressed a concern that the top position of Council 77 would merely continue to be a temporary stopover in the rung of advancement for aspiring union careerists, that concern soon turned out to be decidedly misplaced. By all accounts, Ed Hartman, who assumed the helm of AFSCME in West Virginia, unlike his predecessors, relished his newfound position as executive director of Council 77. Early in Hartman's tenure, the AFSCME statewide affiliate had several area locals of state workers, Local 3248 becoming one of the largest and most active, along with a scattering of municipal locals. Hartman had a background with the brewery workers in Georgia and Texas before landing the job as a union official in West Virginia. He looked the picture of a stereotypical labor boss, heavyset with coiffed hair, given to wearing expensive clothing and known to carry a firearm.

Hartman's singular accomplishment in 2001, after settling into the job, was busting the staff union at Council 77. The Council's United Staff Union (USU) bargaining unit had been small to begin with, consisting of three field representatives and an administrative secretary, owing in no small part to the relatively low density of union membership in West Virginia's state, county, and city government workforces, particularly when seen in contrast to the better organized public education sector unions.[6] In June 2001, Hartman laid off two of the field representatives and then filed a clarification petition with the National Labor Relations Board (NLRB) to have the secretarial position excluded from the staff union bargaining unit on grounds that it involved confidential duties.[7]

As a prelude to a 2002 NLRB ruling on union representation for AFSCME staff, it was revealed that Hartman did not seek or obtain approval from Council 77's executive board for the governing council's membership, largely handpicked by Hartman himself, when he filed the petition to remove the administrative secretary from USU membership. The NLRB decision noted,

> [While] Hartman operates "with the approval of the Executive Board," that body has not engaged in active oversight of his labor relations policy. The president of the Executive Board represents the Employer at second step grievance meetings and in arbitrations, but no one from the Executive Board regularly reviews Hartman's labor relations policies or actions. For example, Hartman independently determined to lay off employees in June 2001 ... and reassigned their duties. Hartman made and executed the decision to hire temporary employees ... Hartman sent a letter terminating the contract and reopening negotiations without notifying or consulting the Executive Board, which met shortly before the letter was

> sent.... The Executive Board has taken no action to countermand him. Additionally, side letters negotiated ... modifying contractual provisions ... were signed only by ... the executive director.[8]

Although, in 2002, the NLRB regional director rejected Hartman's exclusion petition, the incumbent office secretary was so illtreated by Hartman that she had already resigned in October, 2001, and, after replacing the remaining staff, Hartman's autocratic managerial style proceeded without the obstacle of having to honor a staff union contract. Hartman subsequently raised his own salary, moved to more spacious offices, bought new furniture, and terminated remaining staff medical benefits.

In addition to his union busting within the paid staff, providing services to dues-paying members suffered under Hartman's regime, and he repeatedly refused to provide representation in union members' grievances. In one case, for example, Council 77 had been listed as the employee representative in a group grievance, and when that grievance was denied after a lower-level proceeding on January 23, 2003, Hartman neither notified the grievants of having received the adverse decision nor filed an appeal on their behalf.[9] Absent a collective bargaining apparatus in West Virginia state government that would have imposed "union security" through exclusive representation, Hartman's position nevertheless depended on maintaining a certain number of dues-paying members. He could successfully deflect most internal challenges to his control as executive director because any dissatisfied member was likely to be relatively isolated without an opposition base and would likely simply drop their union membership. At the same time, even a gradually dwindling membership would eventually diminish the available funds from which his salary and perks were drawn, particularly after subsidies by the union's international office were cut.

In order to boost the declining membership of Council 77, Hartman directed his only remaining field organizer at the time to do a mass mailing to five thousand highway maintenance employees, encouraging them to join the union in order to be part of a group discrimination grievance. The issue of the grievance arose from the state's July 1, 2005, decision to grant a 25 percent special hiring rate and a 15 percent pay increase for current employees in the selected job classifications of DOH workers in three counties that bordered Virginia in the state's eastern panhandle. The locality pay increase had resulted from legislative concerns that recruiting workers in those counties had been made difficult by higher wages available in the neighboring state.

Hartman's ploy resulted in more than five hundred highway employees signing on as new members, although a few highway workers realized that since any state employee had legal standing to grieve, the grievance board would consolidate separately filed grievances on the same issue into a group for purposes of "judicial economy," thus allowing them to file individually without requiring them to join AFSCME. The grievance board did, however, segment the group grievance by agency districts, for yet additional reasons of judicial economy, and the proceeding for DOH workers in the District 1 case went to hearing first. Three years after the initial filing of the locality pay group grievance, the board's administrative law judge, Denise Spatafore, issued a decision denying it at the final step.[10] AFSCME then filed an appeal with the Kanawha County Circuit Court, and by order entered December 22, 2009, that court affirmed the grievance board's decision. A further appeal to the state supreme court was also unsuccessful.[11] AFSCME did not further pursue the remaining locality discrimination grievances in the other highway districts, although an argument could have been made that the facts relevant to the discrimination claim may have differed from those in District 1 for other districts of the agency.

Hartman was a political player adept at working the state AFL-CIO's organizational structure, and he aligned himself with the state federation's leader, Kenny Perdue, as well as the entrenched leadership of other affiliated unions, which had devised the longstanding arrangement of divvying up state agencies into jurisdictional fiefs. He also went along with the decision by the state labor federation to endorse Joe Manchin's 2005 run for governor. Manchin had a previous record of supporting "right-to-work" bills while holding a seat in the legislature and had been instrumental in undermining the election bid of Charlotte Pritt when, as a labor-backed insurgent, she secured the Democratic nomination for governor in 1996 against the party's establishment. When asked at the state federation's Committee on Political Education convention whether he would, as Pritt had done in 1996, support public employee collective bargaining, Manchin would go no further than to say that he was "open" to the idea. Nevertheless, the state federation, as well as AFSCME Council 77, endorsed Manchin without any apparent hesitation. Kenny Perdue would later even be featured in Manchin's televised political ads.

In 2005, immediately after his election as governor, Manchin created a Commission on Public Sector Employment and Employee Relations, composed of the union bureaucrats that had endorsed him, along with enough businessmen to ensure that its final recommendations would fall short of a collective bargaining proposal. Rather, the commission recommended that the state implement a "meet-and-consult" process by which union employees could periodically advise state agency administrators of proposed recommendations.

On April 9, 2007, more than two years after the commission was convened, Manchin issued an executive order creating a two-year "pilot program" for meet-and-consult panels in selected agencies. AFSCME was allowed to appoint a meet-and-consult panel for DOH. CWA was allowed to appoint a panel for the Division of Corrections, and UMWA was allowed to appoint a panel for the General Services Division. SEIU was reportedly excluded from the meet-and-consult arrangement for having held out for collective bargaining during the Manchin commission process. The only tangible result of any of the panels was a July 1, 2009, uniform policy that provided highway maintenance employees work clothing supplied from a contracted private vendor.[12]

Manchin further demonstrated the actual extent of his gratitude for the support that had been given to him by the

AFL-CIO-affiliated public worker unions when he directed Larry Puccio, his chief of staff, to issue a memorandum imposing a blanket statewide pay freeze on August 26, 2005. Any pay increases, including annual merit raises purportedly based on employee performance evaluations, were placed on indefinite hold. Although there were a few grievances filed by state employees attempting to challenge the action, the unions themselves remained uniformly silent, unwilling to even voice opposition.

In October of 2005, AFSCME Council 77 was scheduled to hold its statewide biennial convention in Charleston. The events leading up to and including that convention became an object lesson in how formal procedures are no assurance that genuine rank-and-file decision-making is being practiced, whatever trappings of representational "democracy" might exist on paper. The majority of the council's executive board owed their positions to Hartman. Whereas on paper the executive director answered to the board; in reality, the board was entirely his creature, a fact that the 2002 NLRB decision had made clear.

Prior to the convention, Hartman had gone separately to various individuals, including board members, that he could reliably count on to do as they were told, and instructed them that as convention chair he would call on them in turn, and they were to dutifully stand and nominate a designed person, or second a prearranged nomination, for each position. Hartman then would close the nomination for a down-the-line voice vote for each board position.

At the convention, Hartman stood at the podium, called it to order, and announced each office for election. He proceeded, keeping his face down with eyes firmly fixed on the notes on the podium, and read his script, "recognizing" by name each person listed without ever looking up. The only glitch occurred when he lost his place at one point and recognized the same individual a second time, at which point she stood up and, to audible laughter from the gathered delegates, nervously and hesitantly proclaimed that she didn't know what she was supposed to say. Hartman quickly recovered his place and continued.

As it was, he had little reason to be concerned that the sham proceeding would go astray, since he had made sure that the delegates present were compliant, if occasionally amused, with the scripted procedure. Hartman had conveniently failed to mail convention notices to any local that he was not confident of being able to control in matters of delegate selection. One such local was AFSCME Local 3268, composed of highway workers in Jackson County.

Local 3268, unlike some AFSCME locals in West Virginia, had a history of member turnout for its monthly meetings and almost every highway worker in Jackson County was a union member. The local also had a track record of lively group discussions and collective problem solving. In one instance, a young new hire had complained at a meeting of always being assigned flagging duty by the boss. Flagging traffic all day on a road job is a genuinely shit job, and someone without much seniority would not necessarily have good cause to complain. But this person was known as a hard worker and his fellow workers in Local 3268 listened to the complaint. In response, fellow workers began to offer to volunteer to take a turn at flagging just to give him a break from the drudgery. The local's president, Bruce Dotson, asked if those volunteers would put their names on a list, which they did.

The day after the local's meeting, Dotson walked into the county administrator's office just before shift began, sat down, and spelled out the new worker's complaint. Before the boss could start to respond, Dotson handed him the list and told him that the logical solution would be to rotate flagging duty with the volunteer workers who had signed. The administrator, as Dotson later put it, didn't see any good reason to piss off the entire crew by disagreeing with their "considered good judgment."

When word got back to Local 3268 that they had been excluded by Hartman from the union's state convention, it was not well received. After the convention, formal charges were brought against Hartman, based in part on Local 3268's disenfranchisement at the state convention. The executive board, whose members Hartman had handpicked, met, as required by AFSCME's "democratic" procedure, to consider his removal. After an apparently empty threat from Hartman to resort to physical violence to settle the matter, along with a significant dollop of red-baiting of any dissent, the board voted in an executive session to retain Hartman as executive director in a nine to one decision.

Dress Code Blues

On August 31, 2005, the DHHR, the agency overseeing state health facilities, announced "Policy Memorandum 2101," a dress code that, among other things, prohibited employees from wearing blue denim jeans at work. The new policy did not specifically restrict employees from wearing denim jeans of any color other than blue, and became effective with revisions on October 1, 2005, but "no exceptions" for blue jeans remained part of the policy.[13]

On April 27, 2006, non–direct care staff at the Beckley nursing home operated by the agency successfully won a grievance challenging the prohibition of wearing blue-colored denim jeans at work on the basis that the policy was arbitrary and capricious.[14] Local 1199 then won another grievance decision on April 28, 2006, on behalf of direct care agency employees at Hopemont Hospital in Preston County, also a state-operated nursing home.[15]

On December 7, 2007, a circuit court judge appointed by Governor Joe Manchin reversed both of the board's decisions in favor of DHHR nursing home workers on appeal. Three days later, the attorney retained by the union sent a letter to union grievants at the Beckley and Hopemont nursing homes expressing the opinion that any appeal to the state's supreme court had a less than likely chance of prevailing. At any rate, Local 1199 never appealed the circuit court reversal. Not long after, SEIU apparently lost any interest in its franchise in West Virginia's state health facilities and "gifted" its membership there to AFSCME.

Parenthetically, it should be noted that a state grievance board judge in 2015 again granted an employee grievance contesting a specific prohibition on wearing blue jeans at work eight years later although the circuit court reversal of 2007 was never appealed.[16] In January 2019, the same Beckley nursing home administrator who had imposed inflexible adherence to the "no exceptions" policy of 2005 issued a directive allowing employees to wear blue jeans on Fridays.

A Group-in-Fusion

Throughout 2006, dissident members of Local 3268 and Local 3248 held conversations and meetings regarding what to do about Hartman's control over AFSCME in West Virginia. As previously noted, Manchin had imposed a wage freeze of an indefinite duration, commonly referred to as the "Puccio memorandum" after his chief-of-staff, Larry Puccio. That measure, along with the privatization of the state's workers' compensation agency, gave every indication that AFSCME's decision to back the Manchin administration meant there would be scant protection against whatever else might come down the road.

By the end of summer of 2006, insurgent members of the two locals had reached a consensus that any further attempt to democratize AFSCME Council 77 was pointless. State workers lacked even an agency shop (so there was no paycheck dues checkoff that union members who were aware of and dissatisfied with Hartman's autocracy could simply stop), a fact that severely limited their chance of building and sustaining a reform faction within the union along the lines of Miners for Democracy or Teamsters for a Democratic Union. Hartman's failure to provide union representation to state workers filing grievances—he was not shy about telling members that there was, in West Virginia, no "duty to represent"—undercut the principal rationale for public employees to join the union, hampering recruitment efforts.

Lacking any realistic option of creating an insurgent caucus within Council 77, by August 2006, a core group from the two locals formed an informal organizing committee for the creation of a West Virginia Public Workers Union (WVPWU).[17] Initially there had been discussion of seeking affiliation, as 1199 had, with the SEIU. That idea was fueled by SEIU president Andy Stern's well-publicized spat with AFSCME and his subsequent 2005 break with the AFL-CIO to set up the rival Change to Win federation.

There were, however, at the same time more than a few indications that SEIU was every bit as mired in the bureaucratic vertical union model as AFSCME, although that realization did not undermine a rough consensus among the dissidents that some sort of affiliation would be advantageous.

What quickly caught the attention of the insurgents were walkouts by city sanitation workers in Raleigh, North Carolina, on September 13 and 14, 2006. The North Carolina work stoppages were also conducted by public workers, striking over issues—such as pay and overtime—that resonated with West Virginians. There was also a shared absence of laws enabling public sector collective bargaining in the two states. Uppermost in the minds of the West Virginians, however, was that the Raleigh municipal workers were striking in a state where both collective bargaining and public worker strikes were explicitly illegal, yet, in defiance of those laws, a group of Black workers had the solidarity and community support to pull off a successful strike.[18] Even the name of the union of the striking workers in Raleigh—the North Carolina Public Service Workers Union (NCPSWU)—was close to the name the West Virginia insurgents had already chosen for themselves.

NCPSWU had its origin in Black Workers for Justice, organizing with state university housekeeping staff in 1997. After unsuccessfully approaching a number of AFL-CIO unions—which had included AFSCME, CWA, and SEIU—NCPSWU affiliated as Local 150 with the independent United Electrical, Radio and Machine Workers of America (UE).[19]

The UE, in turn, had been formed soon after the emergence of the CIO but had left the CIO during the purge of radical unions by John L. Lewis in the Red Scare of the 1940s, years before the CIO merged with the AFL, and UE promoted itself as an independent alternative to the autocratic business unionism of the labor federation.

After discussion of the North Carolina walkout spread among the West Virginia state workers, a decision was made to contact the UE national office in Pittsburgh on behalf of the West Virginia Public Workers Union (WVPWU) and arrange a meeting. On

September 19, 2006, a delegation of three state workers who had been involved in starting the new union, including Local 3268's former president and chief steward, drove from Charleston to Pittsburgh to explore affiliation with UE.

In retrospect, the reasons seem obvious why WVPWU followed the lead of NCPSWU in approaching UE. Under its oft-repeated slogan that "the members run this union," UE presented itself as different from the sort of hierarchical unionism that had repeatedly failed in organizing the bulk of West Virginia's public workers. To cite one historical account, UE "came into existence as a coalition of locally based, independently organized unions. The strength of UE—and its sheer ability to survive—has been based in a democratic structure investing decision making at the workplace level."[20] Moreover, if UE was willing to support Black workers in the antiunion Deep South, maybe it would, as the leftist Local 1199 had been in the 1970s, prove receptive to a group of mostly white Appalachian workers.

WVPWU's initial contact in Pittsburgh had been with UE's then-senior international representative, Gene Elk, who made the September 19, 2006, appointment. Although Elk was the one who greeted the WVPWU delegates when they arrived in Pittsburgh, they were ushered into a meeting with the UE's national officers, president John Hovis, secretary-treasurer Bruce Klipple, and director of organizing Bob Kingsley. The Pittsburgh meeting lasted two hours. The West Virginians described their recent experience, and the UE national officers made a case for why UE was both different from and more democratic than AFL-CIO unions. The conclusion of the conversation was that UE would send organizing staff into West Virginia to assist WVPWU in recruiting members, and, if specific membership goals were met, WVPWU would be granted status as a local in UE.

Shortly after, UE sent national staff in to help leaflet workplaces, distribute membership cards, and stage demonstrations and rallies. In addition to Elk, the national staff sent into West Virginia for extensive durations initially included Karen Hardin, John Thompson, Salia Warren, and Steve Bader. The organizing committee, for its part, engaged in internal workplace organizing, as well as generating community support and considerable media publicity. UE's national office set a graduated schedule for membership sign-ups, which the organizing committee not only met but also repeatedly exceeded.[21]

A WVPWU constitution was drafted, using the North Carolina local as a model. Kingsley insisted that a provision be added that prohibited disaffiliation, saying that it was standard boilerplate language. The union constitution provided that in addition to specific shop organizations, there would be chapters to conduct membership meetings and be the source of delegates for state conventions, analogous in function to the locals of AFSCME's statewide council.

A central provision of the WVPWU constitution involved the creation of a statewide stewards' council to be composed of elected workplace shop stewards. The purpose of shop stewards was not only to handle the initial stages of formal grievance filings, but also to provide day-to-day representation of union members to facilitate the resolution of conflicts with management on the shop floor, convene shop meetings, communicate union concerns to members and, conversely, members' issues and initiatives to the rest of the union at chapter and statewide levels. This structure was meant to provide a means by which the union would not only be relevant to specific workplaces, but would also be responsive to continuous member participation and control and decision-making.

The two initial chapters were entirely drawn from AFSCME Locals 3268 and 3248—DOH chapters based in Jackson County and a state capitol chapter, respectively. Early on, a substantial number of DHHR employees in the Charleston area signed membership cards, and a separate DHHR chapter was also soon established. Although the new organization was initially centered in the Charleston and Jackson County areas, it was not long into the organizing that AFSCME Local 3229—composed of employees of the Parkways Authority, also known as the West Virginia Turnpike—approached the organizing committee to be admitted as a chapter. The workplaces associated with the Parkways Authority extended from the outskirts of Charleston, south to Beckley and Ghent in Raleigh County, and constituted a defined, relatively compact geographical area. It was large enough to comprise a significant membership and close enough in distance to allow member attendance at monthly chapter meetings.

Although Karen Hardin, a national UE staffer assigned to West Virginia, expressed reservations about the parkway workers becoming a chapter, the organizing committee itself had no hesitation in accepting the request. The committee viewed the unsolicited approach by turnpike employees as confirmation that West Virginia public workers wanted "a union of their own choosing." By the end of summer 2007, WVPWU had four functioning chapters.

A delegation from WVPWU led by the new union's first president, Bruce Dotson, attended the UE national convention that fall in Pittsburgh in order to be chartered as UE Local 170 on September 17, 2007.[22] Initially, UE's national office had assigned three of its staffers—Hardin, Thompson, and Warren—to West Virginia on a full-time basis. In addition to visiting workplaces, they spent considerable time on lobbying at the state capitol and attending the organizing committee, and later, executive committee meetings, along with chapter membership meetings. Thompson was assigned to West Virginia by Kingsley specifically to provide training to officers and shop stewards. In order to give staffers a base of operations, the national office rented an apartment on Charleston's east end, close to the state capitol complex and the building that WVPWU had rented as a union hall, as well as to the state's main grievance board offices.

As DOH membership grew throughout the state, Dotson prevailed upon the local's executive committee to approve creation of two additional chapters to accommodate the surge in DOH members, one centered in Clarksburg and a second in the southern counties. The Clarksburg chapter soon shed an exclusively DOH orientation after an influx of new members working in the Division of Rehabilitation Services, which had one of its two largest state offices there.

DHHR, the state's largest state agency by far, proved early on to be a fertile ground for new membership. Like DOH, which was the second-largest agency, DHHR maintained offices throughout the state. From early on, however, national office staff assigned to West Virginia discouraged the creation of either additional DHHR chapters or, as an alternative, chapters based on locality rather than agency, although that model had proved successful in Charleston and Clarksburg. The rationale put forward for this opposition was Hardin's claim that employees in one state agency had "nothing in common" with the employees at another state agency.

There may well have been other reasons for UE national staff to want to maintain a single, statewide chapter for DHHR: it may have derived from the mindset of identifying "bargaining units," which accompanied NLRB-type organizing arrangements. Additionally, Hardin and Thompson made it clear that part of their work on behalf of the national office was to attend union meetings and offer guidance for each chapter. The more chapters the local union formed, the more travel and time would be involved for national staff to attend and ride herd on chapter membership meetings. A counterargument to that, however, was the consideration that the closer monthly chapter meetings were held to where state workers lived and worked, the better the expected member attendance at those meetings. It was one thing to say "the members run this union," it was another to allow and encourage the conditions for that to be the case.

Road Wars

In 1970, one year after the 1969 State Road Commission strike, that agency was reorganized as the West Virginia Department of Highways, at which the time it had nearly ten thousand employees. In 1989, it was again reorganized, this time as the West Virginia Division of Highways and placed under the newly created cabinet-level agency of the West Virginia Department of Transportation, within which were also included the Parkways Authority, the West Virginia Division of Motor Vehicles, and a few smaller agencies. All of those component agencies, aside from Parkways, had by then come into the civil service system. Given the significance of the role played by highway workers in the founding of WVPWU, it was unsurprising that the division would be significant contested terrain for the new union from the outset.

By the time Joe Manchin became governor of West Virginia on January 17, 2005, DOH was a statewide executive branch agency with thousands of miles of roads under its care, divided into ten regional districts throughout the state, and largely funded by federal money supplemented by state resources including a gasoline tax. Under Manchin's directive, a working policy was implemented at DOH that restricted agency operations to what was henceforth referred to as a core maintenance plan (CMP).[23]

Under "core maintenance," the range of acceptable activities allowed were limited to pothole patching, roadside ditching, mowing medians and rights-of-way, and snow removal and ice control.[24] All other work, however much it had been traditionally performed by state highway workers—including bridge maintenance and repair, "major" paving and road construction, road signs, and paint striping of highway lanes—would henceforth be done by private contractors, such as Manchin campaign contributor Turman Construction.[25]

The political expediency for the imposition of "core maintenance" was obvious. DOH was no longer the open preserve for patronage or "spoils" jobs that it had been prior to its admittedly belated inclusion into the civil service system. With the expectation of cash donations collected from employees for an incumbent governor's campaign coffers—what had been euphemistically once known as the "flower fund"—now off the table, sources for political campaign contributions needed to be found elsewhere.

Once highway workers could no longer be reliably shaken down for money, outsourcing road work to private contractors—privatization—was a solution, and awarding private contracts for projects removed from DOH by restricting it to "core maintenance" created an opportunity. Paul Turman, the governor's pick for number two at the Department of Transportation, came from a family-owned firm involved in heavy construction, and the Turman firm was one from which an extensive list of employees, including even low-level office staff, had made the maximum legally allowed contributions to Manchin's gubernatorial fund. Over time, the CMP also allowed the agency to significantly reduce the DOH workforce through normal attrition and turnover.

None of this was lost on state workers. Paul Mattox, the Manchin-designated cabinet secretary in charge of highways, along with Turman, on one occasion paid a visit to the Fayette County DOH garage for a mandatory meeting with employees. After the meeting's conclusion, the two were unpleasantly surprised when they attempted to enter their state vehicle for departure as the door handles were found to have been slathered with grease by persons unknown. When no one would confess to the sabotage, to Turman's reported chagrin, his demand that each and every Fayette County employee be subjected to discipline was determined to be legally unenforceable.

DOH's Equipment Division, headquartered in Buckhannon, operated a facility that included repair shops and a warehouse, as well as a location to conduct any equipment training not offered at the Medina heavy equipment training facility operated under the auspices of the Operating Engineers. In 2006, the Equipment Division was investigated by the West Virginia Ethics Commission and the State Legislative Auditor in what Robert Glen Andrew II, head of that division, dismissed as "malarkey." The results of that investigation were never released.[26]

One of the inevitable results of imposing CMP was that hundreds of pieces of road and construction equipment purchased by state taxpayers were suddenly unneeded and unused by the highways agency. In May, 2007, a few months before WVPWU's chartering as UE Local 170, a public auction was conducted at which more than three hundred pieces of heavy equipment owned by the state were sold and a reported $1.5 million netted.[27] DOH workers complained that newly reconditioned vehicles and heavy equipment were being sold at junk scrap prices to private companies who had been given advance notice on which items to bid. The workers also worried that their jobs were becoming increasingly precarious if the agency no longer owned the equipment needed to do much of the road work.

On August 25, 2007, WVPWU staged a rally at the state capitol to protest DOH privatization and the awarding of "lucrative contracts to political supporters."[28] On September 15, 2007, the union picketed the Buckhannon facility during a second large-scale auction of equipment. One media report of the union campaign stated that a "number of workers contend the sale and the 'core maintenance' program is a smokescreen for privatizing the highway department."[29] A flyer distributed by WVPWU stated:

> Join UE Local 170 members and state highway workers at the Buckhannon Equipment Yard as we protest the Manchin Administration's auction of several million dollars' worth of vital equipment which is necessary to repair our roads. Without this vital equipment, we expect that Gov. Manchin and the Division of Highways will attempt to sell off lucrative contracts to political supporters to repair state roads. Under this privatization scheme, highway workers face layoffs and taxpayers will pay the bill for soaring repair costs."[30]

Imposition of CMP proceeded undeterred by the union's vocal opposition. The reduction in the DOH workforce was similarly unabated and was exacerbated by the stagnant pay scale offered applicants to the diminished number of job postings. Federal grants accounted for 80–90 percent of road construction in West Virginia and on January 2, 2008, federal highway administrators sent a letter to Mattox warning him that funding was in jeopardy due to the "recent trend" in workforce reduction.[31] The letter from the federal highways administration noted a spate of retirements, resignations, and an "inability to attract, replace and retain staff." The DOH response referred to its reliance on "private contractors … to perform work once done by state employees," which prompted the union to counter that the state was engaged in "privatization by stealth."[32] DOH nevertheless conceded that its pay scale was too low to attract new hires, and WVPWU began what proved to be a years-long campaign to address pay for highway employees.

The Members Run This Union

The second annual statewide convention of the WVPWU, UE Local 170, was held on August 23, 2008, preceded by a rally on the steps of the state capitol in Charleston. One major issue addressed was the imposition of the statewide freeze on any pay increases for state workers that had become known as the Puccio memorandum, named after Manchin's chief of staff Larry Puccio, a political operative who authored the pay freeze order, initially imposed August 29, 2005.

WVPWU had filed a grievance on November 26, 2007, on behalf of Carol Roush, a female employee of the DOH contesting a pay discrepancy with her male counterparts. DOH, for its part, argued that they were barred from redressing any pay matters because of the issuance of the Puccio memo by the governor's office. Nevertheless, on July 16, 2008, the state's attorney general issued a decision that found the Puccio memo to be illegal and a matter of executive power overreach, a finding that was subsequently ignored by the executive agencies that answered to the governor. Despite that, the union continued to pursue the grievance to the third step, where it went before the West Virginia Public Employees Grievance Board. Thomas Gillooly, the administrative law judge who heard the case at that level was fired after conducting the hearing—but before he could issue a ruling—in what the union came to view as blatant political interference from the governor's office. Needless to say, when the board eventually issued a decision, the grievance was denied.[33]

The Roush case was ultimately filed as a civil action on September 9, 2009. In a pretrial hearing before Kanawha County circuit court judge Louis "Duke" Bloom on November 10, 2010, DOH again sought refuge for its pay discrimination by invoking the Puccio memo, which it represented as having the force of law. When Bloom countered that it was nothing more than a mere administrative policy, the agency relented to pressure to settle the case.[34] On November 15, 2010, Earl Ray Tomblin succeeded Manchin, now US senator, and became acting governor, and on March 29, 2011, Tomblin's own chief of staff, Rob Alsop, issued a new memorandum essentially and belatedly lifting the infamous Puccio memo.[35]

Another major topic for the 2008 WVPWU state convention was the state of job conditions at the state's hospitals and health facilities. Earlier that year, SEIU Local 1199 had ceased representing state hospital employees and entered into an arrangement turning over its membership in those facilities to AFSCME Council 77. Unhappy with that handover, on June 17, 2008, former 1199 members at Mildred Mitchell Bateman Hospital, a psychiatric facility in Huntington, attended an executive committee meeting of WVPWU, presenting a call for solidarity in the face of chronic and dangerous understaffing. On July 25, 2008, WVPWU conducted a highly publicized protest rally at Bateman that resulted in facility administrators promising an addition of seventy full-time positions to that facility alone, and to take steps to expand facilities to reduce continued overcrowding.

The 2008 convention included a performance by local labor troubadour Elaine Purkey, a veteran of both the Ravenswood steel lockout and the Pittston coal strike. Purkey's rendition of "Solidarity Forever," composed by the Industrial Workers of the World's Ralph Chaplin in the aftermath of the West Virginia coal strike of 1912, was followed by a performance of a new ballad, dedicated to public service workers that Purkey said had inspired the song by the dramatic emergence of the union. The local's constitution was amended by delegates to mandate the election of statewide officers on an annual basis, as a move to strengthen the democratic control of the rank-and-file membership over the union.[36]

The vacuum left by 1199's withdrawal from state hospitals—along with AFSCME's negligent response in its purported designation as SEIU's replacement, first evident at Bateman—became increasingly apparent at other DHHR-operated facilities around West Virginia during 2009. WVPWU meetings not only continued at Bateman but also began taking place at other locations. On April 28, a meeting at Jackie Withrow Hospital in Beckley, formerly known as Pinecrest Hospital nursing home, was well-attended by the ex-SEIU staff there. On May 5, 2009, a meeting was held at Lakin Hospital, a long-term care facility in Mason County.

On June 6, 2009, WVPWU members at Bateman met to form a chapter of the union and requested their own charter as such, duly granted by the local's executive committee on June 9. Recruitment meetings followed at Welch Community Hospital in McDowell County on June 11 and Hopemont, a nursing home in Preston County, on June 16. According to the union's July 2009 newsletter: "We formed our first Hospital Chapter at Mildred Mitchell Bateman and are on target to form new chapters at several hospitals by this fall."[37] In August, recruiting began at William R. Sharpe, Jr. Hospital, in Weston, the largest of West Virginia's state-run psychiatric hospitals.

On the legislative front, the Manchin administration had backed the introduction of a bill that would allow the governor to place state employees on unpaid furlough. It passed the state senate with only one dissenting vote and moved on to committee consideration in the House of Delegates. WVPWU organized a telephone call-in campaign, so successful that it prompted a call to the union by the house speaker with an assurance that the bill was tabled.

On October 10, 2009, the WVPWU state convention was held in Charleston, at which the attending delegates approved a number of procedural and financial constitutional amendments. There was considerable and extended debate, however, on a proposal to increase dues from seventeen to nineteen dollars per month. The proposed increase had originated with UE national office staffers Thompson and Hardin, who had circulated contrasting budgets, one reflecting the existing dues rates and showing an imminent deficit, and the other premised on approval of the increase. The plausibility of the projected budgets was undermined when convention delegates noticed that some items of fixed costs, such as utility expenses, were calculated at greater amounts in the existing budget figures compared to the future budget calculations. The contention that the costs of gas and electric bills, for example, would actually decrease if dues were raised proved to be unpersuasive to the convention delegates.

Additionally, many members argued that higher union dues, even if only one or two dollars, would be inappropriate considering that pay remained frozen under the Puccio memo and that state worker benefits continued to be eroded by administrators such as the Public Employees Insurance Agency (PEIA) finance board. Raising dues, it was argued, would be an impediment to organizing new members considering the low pay for public employees generally. In a vote of the membership in attendance, the dues increase was soundly rejected.

The role played by Thompson and Hardin in pushing for the dues increase, coupled with the clumsiness of the contrasting budget projections circulated on its behalf, left a number of local members with the suspicion that UE's national office was anxious to lay some groundwork to shore up its own financial difficulties, an impression only strengthened by the dire if unrealized predictions of insolvency that national office staff continued to circulate in conversations with members in the months that followed. There were already reports that Thompson and Hardin were prone to exercise heavy-handed control of chapter meetings they that attended and that they spent much of their time cultivating members with whom they would share their "grave concerns" about the direction of the local union. After one executive committee meeting, Hardin told the local's president that she didn't want to "hear that shit about 'the members run this union.'"

Staff interference in the local's governance also became an issue with the operation of the local's office in Charleston. The executive committee minutes for July 21, 2009, recorded that the local's president sought approval to hire office staff for the local. The minutes for August 18, 2009, recorded that Mike Mollohan was hired as office manager for the local. Mollohan would later report that Hardin was frequently getting into the local's financial and membership records and database. On finding out about his report,

Hardin verbally attacked Mollohan, which prompted his resignation. Hardin subsequently took it upon herself to recruit a replacement as the local's office manager; this time she would decide whom to hire, and that person would report exclusively to her.

Having assumed unobstructed control of recordkeeping for the local, Hardin proceeded to assign all new state hospital members to the Bateman chapter, irrespective of their work locations. The local's executive committee, however, had chartered the Bateman chapter as a chapter exclusive to employees of that facility, and the members from other facilities, all of which were scattered across the state at a considerable distance from Huntington, were intended to be temporarily assigned to the statewide DHHR chapter pending formation of their own facility chapters.[38]

In the spring of 2010, Dotson took disability retirement from the state, and, no longer being an active public sector employee, resigned as the union's president. At his suggestion, the executive committee appointed recording secretary Pam Schwarz as interim local president. Schwarz, an employee at the Mason County DHHR, had a long history of union activism, formerly with the Ironworkers, before becoming a state employee. Like all WVPWU officers, she was also a full-time employee of the state, and served as an unpaid volunteer in her spare time.

The absence of Schwarz from the union office during working hours meant that she, like Bruce Dotson before her, was largely unaware of the goings-on in the office during the day, which effectively allowed Thompson and Hardin unfettered access to the local's records. Schwarz had been on the executive committee during the chartering of the Bateman local and was not at first informed that national office staff had placed state hospital workers as a group in the Bateman chapter.

Shortly after Schwarz assumed the WVPWU presidency, the union found itself in a battle to thwart the privatization of the West Virginia Office of Technology (WVOT). In 2005, Manchin transformed an entire agency, the state's Workers' Compensation Commission, into a private insurance carrier, BrickStreet Insurance, and had done so with the tacit approval of AFSCME. Later, the

Manchin administration reorganized the state's computer technology services into a distinct and separate agency, and placed as its director an executive recently with corporate industry. State workers saw a familiar pattern developing. The union responded with publicized rallies and a symposium on privatization. Unfortunately for the Manchin administration, the move had come at a time when similar outsourcing of IT in other states had proved expensive if not disastrous, and there were moves elsewhere to undo and reverse previous privatization. The public outcry against privatization generated by the union's campaign proved successful, and plans for a corporate takeover were finally abandoned by the state.[39]

In the midst of the fight over information technology privatization, at a press conference and rally at the state capitol complex, Schwarz headlined the speakers for assembled protesters and reporters on July 14, 2010. She later complained that Hardin had tried to dictate to her what to say, to which she had at the time responded, "I'm nobody's puppet." The episode was, however, an indication of things to come. When, in 2010, it became known that Hardin had used her access to the union's database to place any and all hospital workers in the Bateman chapter, Schwarz confronted Hardin about her defiance of the local's previous decision. Although Hardin denied any wrongdoing, she and Thompson began to approach various hospital members, including those at Bateman, telling them that Schwarz and the local's leadership were seeking to disenfranchise them. They circulated a petition that accused the executive committee of being opposed to allowing hospital workers a voice in the union, specifically because, as Hardin put it, hospital employees had "nothing in common" with other DHHR employees.

The original vision of WVPWU, embodied in its first chapters at the time of its formation and the subsequent creation of locality-based DOH chapters, was along the lines of AFSCME locals, based on a number of workers in a facility, city, or county sufficient to constitute a viable membership group. That had been the pattern when the parkways chapter had been formed, as it had been when Dotson oversaw the creation of DOH Chapter 2, which became the Clarksburg Chapter on July 7, 2009, after recruiting a sizable membership from the Division of Rehabilitation Services. The clear intention of WVPWU was not only to form chapters for each of the far-flung health facilities, but also to develop the statewide DHHR chapter into components of localized organizations after recruiting a critical mass of members in various areas of the state.

The demand in the petition circulated by Hardin and Thompson, however, was to immediately create a new and separate statewide hospital chapter, and their allegation was that the union's leadership was improperly and undemocratically blocking that goal. Schwarz and the rest of the executive committee were alarmed by national office staff blatantly preempting the local's decision-making and deliberately fomenting discord within the ranks with a concocted claim.

At an executive committee meeting on September 14, 2010, there was, according to the minutes, discussion about a hospital conference that had been scheduled for September 18 by Hardin and Thompson. "Staff was directed to cancel the meeting and, in the alternative, encourage hospital workers to attend the DHHR meeting scheduled for October 7, where they could elect delegates to the convention."[40] According to the September 14, 2010, minutes, "Karen Hardin asserted that hospital workers have nothing in common with the other union chapters, including DHHR. John Thompson stated that meetings had been held with the goal of identifying leaders to establish chapters at each hospital." A motion passed that would allow hospital workers who did not work at Bateman to caucus for the time being as originally assigned, with DHHR, until such time as chapters for each facility were formed. Although Hardin voiced emphatic disagreement with the motion, it was carried by a clear majority vote.[41]

Given the persistence of national staff in undermining the local's decision-making, executive committee members lodged a protest with the national office, citing UE's constitution, Article 25: "Staff members have no right to interfere with UE rank-and-file control, including election processes, at any level of the union. To deviate from this policy would lead to a staff-controlled union."

UE director of organizing Bob Kingsley responded by hurriedly calling a meeting of national office staff in Pittsburgh, but, at the last minute on October 8, 2010, he canceled the meeting and informed WVPWU that Thompson and Hardin had been reassigned to duties outside of West Virginia. On October 12, 2010, Schwarz informed the executive committee that national staff had been reassigned and read aloud Article 25 of UE national constitution. There was discussion of the need to reorganize chapters geographically rather than by continuing statewide single-agency chapters. At the meeting, Bateman's Jay Miser recommended exploring a chapter for Hopemont Hospital, a state-operated extended care nursing home in Preston County.[42]

Schwarz convened the October 30, 2010, statewide WVPWU convention with an announcement that she had recently learned that, in November 2009, a member of UE's national office staff had removed all hospital workers from the database of the DHHR Chapter. Since only Bateman's hospital workers had a defined hospital chapter that conducted meetings, she continued, this removal effectively disenfranchised employees at Lakin and Hopemont nursing homes—who had members in attendance at convention—as well as those at Welch, Sharpe, and Jackie Withrow hospitals, who had no members present.

There was an immediate uproar on the convention floor. First, the petition for the creation of a statewide hospital chapter that had been circulated by national office staff was proffered to the convention by Bateman delegate Jay Miser. The creation of a statewide hospital chapter was moved, seconded, and approved. Then a delegate from Clarksburg, Donna Morgan, angrily demanded to know why Hardin and Thompson had been reassigned. UE's president, John Hovis, attending as a guest, gave a short presentation on Article 25, saying the decision had been made by the national office. In the voting that followed, all of the incumbent executive committee officers were defeated for reelection. Ernie Chafin from DHHR was elected local president, Jennifer Ayers from the Office of Technology was elected vice president, Cathy Miller from the Division of Culture and History was elected as recording secretary, and Jeff Watson was elected chief steward. The purported prior removal of Thompson and Hardin had been a Pyrrhic victory for WVPWU's autonomy.

In an email sent to Pam Schwarz and Steve Thompson on January 26, 2011, recently elected vice president Ayers stated, "The membership at UE Local 170 was not made aware of the misconduct of John Thompson and Karen Hardin prior to our 2010 Statewide Convention and election held on October 30, 2010.... There was merit to the allegations of misconduct by the former executive leadership regarding UE Field Organizers John Thompson and Karen Hardin."[43]

Ayers also wrote that national staffer Thompson had made repeated negative comments regarding the local's previous leadership and throughout the month of September 2010 continually pressed her to run for office. When Ayers expressed reservations about her prospects of winning, Thompson reassured her "not to worry—it was taken care of. He explained that other people were running for offices and he guaranteed that the old leadership wouldn't be re-elected." Ayers continued, "John Thompson persuaded me to run for Vice President. Sometime around mid-September he began encouraging me to run—he said I was a 'natural' and should run for Vice President because I was already doing the political action work. At the time I took it as a compliment. Now I believe he intended to have a puppet Vice President, which I clearly cannot be."[44]

Ayers asserted that she eventually learned, in October 2010, that Thompson had convinced Chafin and Miller to run for office, and that during "the time he and Karen were supposedly removed from West Virginia ... they were here actively promoting their candidates for office." Ayers wrote that she received a voicemail from Thompson instructing her to come to a meeting at Chafin's house on October 16, 2010, to meet Chafin,

> so I could see that she was okay. The meeting at Ernie's house was attended by Ernie, Cathy Miller, John Thompson, Karen Hardin, and myself—John and Karen instructed all three of

> us to meet with the various chapter presidents. John even went so far as to direct me as to what I should be doing with regards to my own IT group—that upset me and I abruptly cut him off and told him that I do not need to be told what to do—I don't wear a leash. Ernie said "well, apparently you can handle yourself."[45]

In Ayers's account of the aftermath of the October 30, 2010, convention, Thompson

> actively sought to control the agenda of the first executive committee (held) on November 9, 2010. He called me soon after the election—sort of in a panic—and asked if I would call Ernie to make sure she made a closed agenda. John said we should not allow any new business to be discussed or brought up because he felt the old leadership would try something. In hindsight, I think John was worried that allegations of election tampering were going to be brought by the former leadership.[46]

According to Ayers, on December 1, 2010, then-director of organizing Kingsley and regional president Andrew Dinkelaker came to Charleston to meet with the local's new executive committee. Ayers attempted to contact Kingsley by telephone message and email prior to the December 1 meeting, but received no response. In addition to Ayers, Chafin, Miller, and Walker, the only attendees at the December 1 meeting were Kingsley and Dinkelaker. In Ayers' email, she wrote,

> Kingsley said John Thompson was going to be assigned to UE Local 170 to work specifically on training and to focus on formation of a statewide hospital chapter. To date, Ernie has not enforced John's assigned duties—I would go so far as to say she condones and encourages his continued interference within UE Local 170. For all intents and purposes, the December 1st meeting was just a dog and pony show. Kingsley and Dinkelaker like the idea of having control over Local 170.[47]

In her email, Ayers wrote that although she faulted the previous leadership for not taking concerns about staff interference to the membership, she nevertheless favored a vote by the membership to restore them to their offices. "Since being elected," she wrote, "I have personally experienced what it means to be on John Thompson's 'bad side' and his ability to manipulate Ernie Chafin (his friend) and others. There hasn't been a moment's peace since I requested the executive committee have an open investigation of the allegations to bring everything into the light of the membership. This effort was actively quashed by Ernie Chafin, Cathy Miller, and DHHR President Ray Greenwood," Ayers continued. "Ernie cannot seem to function in a meeting without having visual cues or input from John. I question who is actually leading Local 170." Ayers concluded her email by stating that it would be best for WVPWU if Thompson and Hardin were permanently removed from West Virginia because they had only sought to make the local "dependent" on them, and "this only ends with UE National having a position of control over a Local."[48]

Ayers's email was too little, too late, and she soon found herself marginalized, vilified, and powerless to reverse the course of events in which she had played, however unwittingly, a role. The statewide hospital chapter championed by national office staff proved unviable and was eventually abandoned in favor of locality-based chapters. The once thriving capitol chapter was split up into two separate chapters, both of which became inactive for lack of attendance sufficient to meet a quorum, even when merged back together years later. State employees in the state capitol area, arguably the largest concentration of public employees in West Virginia, never regained a working forum for membership participation. From 2010 onwards, the UE national office had a compliant if languishing, local in West Virginia.

Return of the Road Wars

Although WVPWU had requested the state legislature to adopt a new pay scale for DOH and to institute a step-raise system comparable to that of federal employees, DOH opted to develop a fifty-page "Transportation Worker Apprenticeship Program" (TWAP) that realigned the "transportation worker" job classification series, which was approved by the State Personnel Board (SPB) on November 18, 2014. TWAP, styled as a "tier" program, was initially put in place with incremental and decidedly mixed results, and DOH returned to SPB three times with revisions from July to September 2015. Numerous grievances were filed charging that the pay policy was arbitrary and capricious in its conception and execution.

A large number of DOH employees were classified in the transportation worker job series, but there were hundreds of others, from clerical workers to engineers, that were not recipients of any benefit from TWAP, a fact that continued to hamper agency operations. In 2017, legislation was passed that required a comprehensive pay plan from the agency. In 2019, after no plan was forthcoming, WVPWU filed a grievance that grew by year's end to more than four hundred employees. The union also drafted a two-page step raise plan with a new pay scale after DOH complained that they didn't know how to comply with the legislative mandate.[49]

Shortly before the prolonged fight over pay scales had begun with the flawed implementation of TWAP, a back story was brewing in the aftermath of the equipment sales that WVPWU had contested at the time of the union's inception. On August 21, 2013, raids based on federal search warrants took place at DOH's Buckhannon equipment division facility, as well as the Cambridge, Ohio, offices of MoTrim, a mowing equipment contractor for the state agency.

By January 2014, Andrew, the sixteen-year head of DOH Equipment Division, was reassigned as a special assistant to West Virginia Department of Transportation cabinet secretary Paul Mattox. That same year, Andrew was the beneficiary of a $10,056 compensation time buyout, the second highest among executive officials that totaled $242,778.[50]

On February 20, 2014, DOH supervisor Barry D. Thompson was indicted for lying to federal investigators and later charged with repairing and replacing parts on a dump truck, using state time and money, that had been already sold at an equipment division auction. On March 7, 2014, Edward Matthew Tuttle, DOH Equipment Division, Buckhannon, and Upshur County DOH administrator, was indicted for lying to federal investigators about the 2011 illegal transport to Baltimore of a dump truck already sold at auction.[51] On August 13, 2014, Tuttle pleaded guilty to lying to federal agents investigating equipment sales.[52] By August 22, 2014, Andrew had resigned from his position as special assistant to Mattox, although DOH employees reported that he was still showing up regularly at the agency's main offices in building 5 of the statehouse complex.

On September 1, 2015, Andrew was charged in a twenty-nine-count indictment by US district attorney William Ihlenfeld for having created a "culture of corruption." Among the charges was using state employees to collect campaign funds and erect political signs for the 2011 election campaign of Earl Ray Tomblin, Manchin's successor as governor. He was also accused in the indictment of rigging bids, illicit sale of state vehicles and equipment, falsifying documents, witness tampering, and collusion with a vendor to secure a "lucrative contract."[53]

The charging document against Andrew stated that from January 2009 to August 2014, Andrew and others participated in a scheme to defraud the State of West Virginia:

> Andrew abused his position of trust as an employee by engaging in illegal activities for the purpose of enriching himself. Andrew prepared, and directed subordinates to prepare, non-competitive bid specifications which favored particular vendors and which did not seek to obtain the best value for the State of West Virginia. Andrew violated, and directed subordinates to violate, terms and conditions of existing contracts with vendors. Andrew solicited a vendor to increase a bid after the bid had closed. Andrew received a bribe from this vendor to salvage better-than-salvage materials. Andrew used state resources, including employees and equipment; to engage in political activity on state time. Andrew violated, and directed others to violate, the statutes

> and regulations which govern the use and disposition of federal excess property by selling, and directing others to sell, the property.[54]

Later that evening, Andrew was found dead in a vehicle at a car wash near Bridgeport, along with a note and shotgun.[55]

Organizing by Grievance

One of the chief complaints that had motivated the workers who initially formed WVPWU had been the continual failure of Council 77 to represent members in the grievance procedure. Yet, without collective bargaining at the state level, filing and fighting grievances were the most obvious available legal mechanisms for building an active public workers union in West Virginia.

The first statewide grievance mechanisms for public school employees had been established by the legislature in 1985, in order "to provide a simple, expeditious and fair process to resolve grievances at the lowest possible administrative level."[56] There was no question that, given the density of union membership in the state's school systems, the triad of AFT, WVEA, and WVSSPA had a measure of clout with lawmakers, especially after the 1980 walkouts.

In 1988, a parallel grievance procedure was established for civil service state employees under the umbrella of a single grievance board. In 1998, legislative revisions were enacted that expanded the grievance board's authority over procedural matters that included a default provision should an employer fail to issue a timely response. At that time, the procedure consisted of four steps, the first three within the employing entity or agency, and the final step was a hearing conducted by full-time administrative law judges working directly under a board appointed by the governor. Administrative law judges were required to be licensed attorneys without an outside practice. The board at the time had offices in Charleston, Morgantown, Wheeling, Beckley, and Elkins, and was issuing more than five hundred decisions and orders annually.

The formation of WVPWU coincided with a comprehensive overhaul of the grievance procedure. In 2007, the legislature abolished the West Virginia Education and State Employees Grievance Board, replacing it with the Public Employees Grievance Board.[57] The new union seized on the changes in grievance law as a terrain upon which to contest the administrative authority of public employers. It was no accident that two of the three delegates sent to the initial meeting with UE in Pittsburgh were shop stewards.

The statutory provisions governing employment in public schools and those applied traditionally to civil service state employees are somewhat distinct from one another in West Virginia state law. As such they tended to reflect the disparity in union density between the two public sector areas. Provisions for seniority rights, for example, had long been more explicit and better defined for public school workers than for employees of state agencies. Rules governing employee grievances, however, were codified under a unitary authority designated as the Education and State Employees Grievance Board.

The grievance law, dating from 1998, as it applied to state workers, mandated a four-step process. Any grievance filed was first heard by the grieving employee's immediate supervisor, and any denial was appealable to a higher authority in the division, and then to the designated departmental administrator. After a denial of the grievance at that level, it could be appealed to an administrative law judge of the grievance board. From there, either party could appeal to the "circuit court of the county in which the grievance occurred," and then to the State Supreme Court of Appeals.

In 2006, meetings conducted by the state legislature's Committee on Government Organization began, under pressure from labor organizations, a thorough reconsideration of the existing grievance procedure. Several of the changes made, some of which would prove significant for subsequent efforts to organize among state workers in particular, were codified in a new statute that was enacted, effective June 30, 2007.[58] One change, which had been sought principally by the education sector unions, was to mandate that all appeals beyond the grievance board go first to the circuit court in Kanawha County, home of the state capital and the county with the most sitting judges. The reasoning seems to have been that, at least in some parts of West Virginia, the county board of education and the county circuit court had politically close connections to the prevailing local political machine and was consequently not regarded as a fair arbiter of disputes involving school district personnel.

Another major change, one that affected state workers and school employees alike, was that the new procedure streamlined the steps involved in a grievance. Under the new formula, the first grievance step was either an informal conference or a formal hearing—the choice was the employee's—conducted by the employer. If denied at the first level, the grievance could be appealed to the newly created West Virginia Public Employees Grievance Board for mediation. If mediation was unsuccessful, the grievant could appeal to a third level hearing before an administrative law judge who would render a written decision. Disciplinary grievances that involved a loss of pay, however, could be filed directly to the third level.

Additionally, the grievance board itself was mandated to have five members appointed by the governor, although it was stipulated that one be from "the largest labor organization in the state," and another from "an education employee organization." In practice, the first labor representative was generally interpreted as a member of the state federation of the AFL-CIO, and was most often the pick of the AFT.

The 2007 grievance law was, at least in language, more employee-friendly than the 1998 statute. One provision that turned out to be at least potentially useful for the various public worker unions was a provision that allowed any public employee the right to designate a representative to be present at any meeting that could discuss or result in disciplinary action, something akin to the *Weingarten* right long enjoyed by private sector union members, along with provisions that rendered illegal any obstruction or retaliation for the exercise of that right. There was, however, no *Miranda* warning explicitly obligated, meaning that the burden of invoking that right was entirely dependent upon the employee's awareness of the law. If, however, collective bargaining was to remain indefinitely off the table for most public employees in West Virginia, the newly enacted statutory right to representation—able to be exercised even before the filing of a grievance—was a tool for organizing of which public sector unions could avail themselves.

Under the sweeping changes of the new law, the four-step process was replaced by three levels. The first step was a hearing or, alternately, an informal conference held with the employing school board or public agency, the second step was a mediation conducted by the board, and the third was a formal hearing before an administrative law judge, who would issue a written decision. The time limit for filing a grievance was changed from ten to fifteen working days. In the view of the union, however, the most significance provision in the new law was the inclusion of the right of an employee to representation not only at every step of the grievance procedure, but also in any meeting with management that could result in disciplinary action.[59]

In a case styled as *Swiger v. West Virginia Civil Service Commissioner*, the state's supreme court had previously upheld the denial of a representative to an employee in a predisciplinary investigation meeting, because the statute covering the meetings at that time only allowed the employees facing possible discipline to appear personally and to reply to charges made against them. Under *Swiger*, the court's majority stated that "if the Legislature wishes to provide due process rights to union representation before termination, it may amend the statute."[60] By instituting a new grievance law in 2007, the legislature did precisely that.

In order to impose disciplinary action on a civil service employee, public entities are generally required to first conduct a "predetermination" meeting with the employee.[61] In the private sector, the right to demand the presence of a union representative at such a meeting is called a *Weingarten* right. Until 2007, such a legal right did not exist for West Virginia public workers, however, and the union saw it as a tool in the struggle against management.

There were definite limitations to that tool. The vast majority of grievances were historically decided against employees, with the administrative law judges wedded to the conservative legal principle of giving deference to prior decisions and, for the greater part, wary of the kind of jurisgenesis willing to grant recognition to workers' rights rather than employers' interests.[62] Additionally, unlike *Miranda* rights in criminal law, the employee was given no affirmative notice of the right and had to invoke it in predisciplinary meetings by an explicit request.

One of the earliest grievances addressing representation rights under the new law resulted in a highly restrictive interpretation of when and under what conditions the right could even be exercised.[63] In that case, a DHHR employee was summoned before an investigative interview by the agency's Office of the Inspector General to answer questions about missing money. When her request for a union steward was denied, the subsequent grievance contesting that action was similarly denied by the grievance judge, based on the statute's wording having no explicit reference in its language to investigatory interviews. According to the judge's ruling: "Investigatory interviews were not included in the short list given in *West Virginia Code* §6C-2-3(g). Since this phrase was removed before the statute was enacted, the undersigned Administrative Law Judge cannot conclude this right was the intent of the Legislature."[64]

The union, however, chose to continue to assert the representation right and found a more expansive decision the following year.[65] In *Koblinsky v. Putnam County Health Department*, an administrative law judge concluded that simply calling a meeting convened by management an "investigatory interview" could not be allowed to get around a worker invoking her right. The judge in *Koblinsky* wrote: "The Legislature expressed that desire in passing *West Virginia Code* §6C-2-3(g) which states that employees are entitled to a representative at any such meetings." The clear reasoning behind this statutory expression of public policy was stated by Justices McGraw and McHugh in their *Swiger* dissenting opinion as follows:

> In *City of Marion v. Weitenhagen*, 361 N.W.2d 323, 328 (Iowa App.1984), the court commented that, "[T]here is nothing in

> the nature of a public employee's work which would result in harm to the public if he or she is given such representation … the public is best served by staunch protection of fundamental rights of expression, association, and petition.
>
> That position is bolstered by other cases that have held that West Virginia's Due Process Clause requires presentation of charges and some opportunity for the employee to respond to them before the imposition of a discipline which deprives the employee of wages or salary.… In passing *West Virginia Code* §6C-2-3(g)(1), the Legislature established that the right to a representative at such meetings is included in those Due Process protections.[66]

WVPWU publicized *Koblinsky* as the equivalent of *Weingarten* for public workers in West Virginia. As the state's largest agency, DHHR was not content to let the matter go away, DHHR had been the only entity to voice opposition to representation rights in the legislative committee hearings that preceded the passage of the new law, and even after that passage had formalized written "Representation Guidelines" that expressly disallowed representation in agency-conducted investigations.

A group grievance from the largest state-operated health facility, Sharpe Hospital, was undertaken by the union after the agency continued to apply its restrictive guidelines.[67] The decision in *Beaton* found that DHHR's guidelines were contrary to law. "Respondent's distinction between an investigatory and a predetermination meeting is an arbitrary and capricious fiction. To the extent that *Knight* … ruled otherwise, it is expressly overruled."[68] *Beaton* was shortly followed by another decision that found the agency had failed to afford "the due process of an interview with a representative to explain or defend her conduct against possible disciplinary action."[69]

CHAPTER 6

The 2010s

Limits to Organizing by Grievance

The continued use by the West Virginia Public Workers Union (WVPWU) of the grievance procedure and its campaign through the state grievance board to implement and expand the right of representation under *Koblinsky* were not only met with opposition from state agencies such as West Virginia's Department of Health and Human Resources (DHHR) and Division of Highways (DOH). They also began to generate new attention in conservative and antilabor political and legal circles.

The West Virginia State Bar, by way of its Unlawful Practice of Law Committee (UPOLC), began considering objections to union employee representatives in the grievance procedure. For their part, state agencies and other public entitles almost universally relied on lawyers, at least by the time a public employee grievance reached the third and final step of the grievance process, which consisted of an administrative hearing before one of the grievance board's judges. Whether the employing agency utilized an attorney working for the state's attorney general's office, a staff attorney already employed by the agency, or a lawyer hired from a private firm, a taxpayer funded government bureaucracy would, of course, have deeper pockets in obtaining legal assistance than a public worker. This fact did not prevent, in at least one instance, one public agency director from hiring a notoriously antilabor law firm whose legal bills literally bankrupted the agency in question, the Putnam County Health Department.[1]

However, not only were agency-paid lawyers occasionally bested by union representatives in grievance decisions, attorneys were being at least theoretically deprived of potential income by union members using shop stewards in adjusting grievances. Since the cost of hiring a lawyer was not a realistic option for most public employees, any push to have nonlawyer representation made unavailable to public workers in filing grievances would serve to effectively remove a major drawing card from unions in the state public sector's non–collective bargaining context. The campaign to have grievance representation declared as a "unlawful practice of law" was therefore, from the outset, an attack on public workers' rights.

On June 5, 2015, UPOLC voted to investigate the issue of nonlawyer representation in administrative hearings and conducted a public hearing on the matter on September 3, 2015. More than a hundred people attended the public hearing and according to a newspaper account: "An overwhelming majority of speakers … sent a clear message to the West Virginia State Bar's Unlawful Practice of Law Committee that nonlawyers should continue to appear as advocates in state administrative proceedings." E. Taylor George, a private lawyer who had been hired as outside counsel for a grievance with the West Virginia Public Service Commission was one of only two presenters who spoke in favor of banning union stewards from grievance proceedings. Twenty speakers, including lawyers from the United Mine Workers of America, American Federation of Teachers, West Virginia Education Association, and the AFL-CIO, as well as individuals from Legal Aid, West Virginia Advocates, and WVPWU all made arguments in favor of allowing nonlawyer representation in administrative hearings.[2]

Nevertheless, on July 12, 2018, UPOLC filed a report with the West Virginia Supreme Court of Appeals recommending that the court prohibit the use of nonlawyer union stewards in grievance hearings. On November 19, 2019, the court issued a response declining to implement the bar's recommendation challenging the existing statutory allowance for union stewards in administrative matters, unless and until there was "an actual case or controversy" before the court, leaving the door open to a future ruling, thereby deferring the question. Given the conservative composition of the court, later seen in its majority decision to uphold passage of right-to-work legislation, along with the 2020 unsuccessful introduction of a law restricting the public worker grievance representation, the prospects of removing employee rights remained on the political agenda of the state's political establishment.

Perhaps mindful of which way the political winds were blowing, the state grievance board soon issued employee-adverse decisions to the clear benefit of serial offender DHHR. In one, an administrative law judge resurrected the same sort of restrictive reasoning that had been relied upon in the previously overturned *Knight* decision, this time to require a union steward to expend annual leave in order to represent a coworker in a predisciplinary meeting, despite the coworker's clear statutory right to request representation.[3] In yet another, a judge fined DHHR a grand total of one dollar for having deliberately and egregiously violated an employee's due process right to requested representation—as well as leaving in place the agency's unlawful discharge of the employee imposed after an unpaid "investigatory" suspension that had inexplicably lasted ten months.[4]

Fighting state power through grievances, however stacked the odds might be in favor of state authority, was the one concrete activity that union members could and did undertake. For example, between July 1, 2007 and June 29, 2008, 1,790 grievances were filed during the first year of the new procedure. Since then, dozens of cases of wrongful discipline, from reprimands to discharges from employment have been successfully fought, in addition to challenges to working conditions and pay that were shown to arbitrarily violate policy and law.

One of the difficulties attendant to a strategy of organizing by grievance was the need to build a stewards council and to continually recruit and train shop stewards. Without achieving and maintaining the capacity to handle a caseload of a hundred or so grievances in play at one time, however, any "organizing by grievance" strategy was impractical. The purported rationale for national staffer John Thompson's original assignment to West

Virginia, as well as for his return after his removal in 2010, was to conduct training, a significant component of which included steward's training. It was even possible that Thompson's eventual elevation to "education director" for the national union was predicated upon that assignment. It was a task, however, that he rarely fulfilled during his assignment in West Virginia, and, given the turnover in state employees, United Electrical (UE) Local 170 was almost never near to having enough stewards for the ongoing caseload, irrespective of James Matles's oft-cited dictum that "no shop grievance is too small."[5] As a longstanding issue, it was evident from early on that UE's national office was not going to follow through with the repeatedly promised training for the local, and so development of a statewide stewards council, despite the prominence of that provision in the local's constitution, never materialized during the local's affiliation with UE.

The original vision of the founders of WVPWU, made evident in the union's constitution, was premised on two principal themes. The first was an explicit intention to create an organization that would be controlled by the members themselves through monthly meetings of chapters. The second was a related principle, somewhat more implicitly stated, that involved a working strategy of "organizing through grievances." For those founders who had broken with the American Federation of State, County and Municipal Employees (AFSCME) in 2006, a major dissatisfaction had been Council 77's abject failure to use the public employee grievance system as a vehicle to contest state power in the workplace. The AFSCME locals that had been the initial core for creating WVPWU had been precisely those with a track record of shop stewards who made a practice of filing formal workplace grievances and representing workers. The statewide AFSCME council had, in contrast, a pattern of either discouraging grievances or failing to provide staff representation for AFSCME members.

In a state in which the vast majority of public workers had no recourse to collective bargaining, much less a legally recognized right to strike, public worker unions are compelled to seek employee power in a limited number of ways. In Texas, for example,

Texas Public Employees Union, affiliated with the Communication Workers of America (CWA), made the strategic decision to use statehouse lobbying as the means by which to recruit members and exert some power on behalf of those members, and, consequently, to neglect grievance adjustment. In West Virginia, a similar emphasis on political influence-building was obvious in not only AFSCME, but also in the CWA local for state correction personnel. WVPWU, however, was begun as an attempt at an alternate model focused on workplace struggle, using grievance adjustment as a strategy to accelerate that struggle.[6]

WVPWU's constitution envisioned not only elected stewards for each chapter, but also the recruitment of shop stewards in workplaces and agencies with sufficient member density, and the eventual development of a statewide stewards council to coordinate day-to-day contestation of managerial authority in the workplace. Such an arrangement would facilitate the ability of members to file and fight grievances as part of a larger organization of workers rather than as individual litigants in a state-sponsored grievance process. The prospect of a functioning network of stewards, however, depended upon additional factors, the most important of which was the creation of active, viable chapters that met frequently and that were genuine forums of continuing membership participation. The role that had been played by national staff assigned to West Virginia by UE had significantly obstructed autonomous organizational development at both the chapter and shop levels. The practical result was poorly attended chapter meetings that were usually dominated by national staff. By retarding the development of functioning chapters, the statewide executive committee became the de facto decision-making body of the union. And, just as the executive board of AFSCME Council 77 had devolved into the creature of its executive director, WVPWU's executive committee was inevitably the creature of UE national staff. The formal mechanism of union "democracy," under UE no less than under AFSCME, masked the verticality of control from the top.

In order to pursue grievance fights on a frequent and sustained level, continuous and accessible steward training would have been necessary, and providing just that level of training had been the long-purported purpose of John Thompson's assignment to West Virginia by the UE's national office. During his extensive time in West Virginia, Thompson never implemented the repeatedly promised intensive program of steward training, and was seemingly content to spend his time either running executive committee and chapter meetings, or cruising around the statehouse during legislative sessions, making himself indistinguishable from other lobbyists. Without a sustainable stewards council capable of handling a substantial caseload, any strategy of organizing by grievance was bound to fail. Without democratic participation and control by the membership, however, no relevant and effective stewards council would develop. The next eruption of public workers insurgency in West Virginia would take yet another form altogether.

School Service Personnel

The public school strikes of 2018 and 2019 in West Virginia were considerably larger than either the 1980 and 1990 teacher strikes, due in no small part to the participation of nonteaching employees such as bus operators; cooks and cafeteria workers; school district clerical staff and secretaries; custodial, grounds, and maintenance workers; school librarians and nurses; teacher aides; counselors; and all the myriad support staff required for public education. Under West Virginia state law, there are, apart from bureaucratic administrators, two groups of public school employees: "professional" employees, that is to say, certified classroom teachers, and "service personnel"—meaning just about everyone else, including bus operators; maintenance, grounds, and custodial workers; cooks; secretarial staff; teacher aides; school librarians—with each of the two respective groups having its own distinct statutory rules as well as classifications and pay scales. Although the working-class status of teachers had in times past been an issue of contention, the blue-collar status of service personnel has understandably been less so. Despite the almost universal tendency of observers to refer to the 2018 and 2019 walkouts as "teacher strikes," the participation by nonteaching school employees was a new and crucial factor in those events.

Founded in 1965, the West Virginia School Service Personnel Association (WVSSPA) exhibited during its early years an ambivalence between being an "employee association" and a union, perhaps a reflection of its origin in and initial affiliation with the West Virginia Education Association (WVEA), and the first and longtime executive secretary of WVSSPA, Kenneth Legg, had been originally a staff lobbyist for WVEA. That initial organizational connection remains evident even today in the constitutional structure of WVSSPA by way of county-based locals, although during the 1970s relations between the two groups became strained as WVEA began to take on more of the features of a union supportive of collective bargaining and eventually exhibited the willingness to exercise the strike tactic while WVSSPA continued to entrench its tactics in the political lobbying and deal-making that was Legg's forte.[7] WVSSPA continued its stated opposition to collective bargaining well into the 1990s and so did not join the 1990 school teacher strike. In an April 19, 1991, interview, Legg informed Phil Edwards that WVSSPA had severed ties with WVEA just at the time that WVEA was moving toward traditional union positions.[8]

Legg retired in 2004, and under a new executive secretary, Bob Brown, WVSSPA began to develop ties with Brown's own previous organizational affiliation, the American Federation of Teachers-West Virginia (AFT-WV). After the two organizations informally collaborated in the effort to restore public school employees into the preexisting pension plan, and away from an untenable market scheme option, Brown maneuvered WVSSPA toward a more formal affiliation with AFT-WV. This had the effect of bringing the 7,800-member school service personnel organization into alignment with the 7,200-member state teachers union that had a national affiliation in AFT as well as membership in the AFL-CIO state federation. The merger, nevertheless, was relatively short-lived; in 2016, with a new executive director, Joe White, who had been hired two years before, WVSSPA voted to sever its relationship with AFT-WV and a turf war for service personnel recruitment predictably broke out between the two groups.[9] So it was that, by 2018, the majority of employees in West Virginia's fifty-five county public school districts, easily the most densely organized part of the state's public sector, were again largely divided between memberships in WVEA, AFT-WV, and WVSSPA.[10]

The 2018 Public School Strike

The separation of public school employees into three distinct and competing unions allowed state legislators to play those groups against one another. WVEA member Jay O'Neal recalls that, in May of 2017, rank-and-file members began expressing frustration at the rivalry between union leaderships and the lack of political leverage that resulted. According to O'Neal, that "realization spurred me to create a Facebook group called 'West Virginia Teachers UNITED,' hoping that it would be a space where teachers could work across unions to make our legislature listen. I added teachers from across the state who I knew were interested in making change and asked them to add others."[11] One of those recruited early on was Brendan Muckian-Bates, a WVEA "building representative" (union steward) who caught O'Neal's attention because of his July 2017 article about the growing discontent among teachers, which appeared in an online publication of the International Socialist Organization.[12] According to one account, in October 2017, O'Neal reposted a news item about a strike in Fresno. One response observed that public worker strikes were illegal in West Virginia, which prompted O'Neal to mention the 1990 strike, which thereafter became a recurrent topic of online conversation.[13]

After repeatedly running up against entrenched union officials whose vested interests were in tamping down anything beyond mere talk about any form of direct action such as strikes, school employees in West Virginia like O'Neal—similar to teachers in Kentucky, Oklahoma, and Arizona during this period—had resorted to creating and using closed Facebook groups as a vehicle by which to organize, agitate, and build a base of solidarity for rank-and-file driven actions. Education labor activist Lois Weiner was involved in some of these efforts and has pointed to the earlier precedent of the use of a Facebook group in January 2016, to organize a "sickout" protest by teachers in Detroit, Michigan.[14]

The significance that West Virginia's labor history played in the subsequent events is evidenced in discussions at the time, even beyond those conducted on the Facebook site. Jane Slaughter, for example, noted the public school struggle drew not only explicitly from the early twentieth-century coal mine wars—evidenced in the widespread symbolic practice of wearing a red bandana—but also in the still-remembered miners' wildcat strike wave that spread across West Virginia throughout the 1970s.[15] The organizers and activists involved in what would eventually become the 2018 West Virginia public school strike would explicitly and repeatedly cite the 1990 teacher strike as an inspiration for what they were undertaking.[16] Throughout 2017, the new Facebook group grew by the hundreds, and the November round of statewide Public Employees Insurance Agency (PEIA) hearings became a recruiting ground for new members. The agitation around the PEIA also prompted the Facebook group to change its name to West Virginia Public Employees UNITED, as state employees were also harmed by diminished PEIA coverage and other adverse legislative initiatives.[17] By that time, union officials in WVEA had learned of the Facebook group and were apparently caught off guard by the grassroots effort to agitate for a strike.

When those posting on the website, amid recurring discussions about the 1990 strike, suggested a plan to swamp the state legislative session for a January 15, 2018, Martin Luther King Jr. Day lobbying blitz, WVEA union leadership decided to co-opt the event. This did nothing, however, to quell the increasing talk of the need for a new strike. WVEA president Dale Lee showed up at the MLK Day rally and tried to tamp down the talk of a strike by insisting that any strike would require a great deal of preparation, which, in one account, only emboldened attending activists to return to their workplaces and accelerate mobilizing for an eventual walkout.[18] In January 2018, the Facebook group had 1,200 members and discussion of an impending strike seemed to energize the effort, so that within a month the group's membership had grown to 21,000.

Kate Endicott, a Mingo County teacher recalls the anger that was ignited when four legislators proposed a bill that would double employee medical costs, a move protested in a social media video by two Mingo teachers posted on the Facebook page. "Outrage turned to action," Endicott notes, "when Mingo County union leaders called for a county-wide meeting open to members from all three unions: the National Education Association, American Federation of Teachers, and West Virginia Service Personnel. This act of unity surprised and emboldened educators from across the county. When the meeting was publicized, educators from other counties started demanding meetings. Quickly, leaders in over seven counties arranged emergency meetings. Teachers and staff were unifying and mobilizing across the state." On January 23, 250 Mingo County school employees from the three unions conducted a three-hour meeting and the sentiment was clearly militant and unified.[19] As strike talk among the rank and file escalated, WVEA locals in four southern counties—Mingo, McDowell, Wyoming, and Logan—met to vote in favor of a one-day walkout.[20] The response of those workers in the southern counties emboldened education employees across the state, such as Eastern Panhandle teacher Jessica Salfia.[21] More counties conducted strike authorization votes, leading the two teacher unions to convene in Flatwoods on February 11 to authorize a statewide walkout, followed by a similar vote by the school service personnel union on February 14. On Saturday, February 17, a large rally of ten thousand was held on the steps of the state capitol in a heavy rain as legislators met inside, and officials of all three education unions announced a two-day state walkout to begin on Thursday, February 22.[22]

According to one account,

> West Virginia's first day out on what was meant to be a two-day strike was as invigorating as it was frightening. An estimated five thousand individuals met at the capitol to protest the mediocre reforms to educators' and public employees' insurance that had been put forth by state legislators and the dangerous pro–school privatization measures

> that were still being considered. Protesters demanded long-term funding for the state's Public Employees Insurance Agency (PEIA) and a larger raise for all public employees. Kym Randolph, West Virginia Education Association (WVEA) director of communication, recounted the long lines at the capitol, with some waiting for more than two hours to make it inside the capitol building to make their voices heard. "The place was packed," Randolph said. "It was very loud. That is by far the largest crowd inside the Capitol in a long, long time."[23]

Jim Justice had been Joe Manchin's pick to become governor. A billionaire coal operator and owner of the luxury Greenbrier Resort hotel, Justice wasted little time in changing his party affiliation from the Democratic to the Republican Party after becoming governor. When the school strike did not end after two days, he flew around the state to conduct meetings about the strike, in hopes of persuading the strikers to return to work. On Monday, February 26, Justice held a town meeting in Wheeling where he told a crowd of educators to go back to the classroom. Rejecting the proposal for a natural gas severance tax to fund public education, Justice instead promised a task force to study the problem of PEIA viability. When an audience members pushed back on his presentation, Justice referred to the crowd as "redneck" and was met with boos.[24]

The next day, February 27, Justice went to Martinsburg for another town meeting, which he began by asking whether anyone was going to shoot him, an indication of the reception he anticipated. Later, at a full auditorium in Morgantown, Justice again squared off against a hostile audience and again he dismissed demands for increased public education funding, and voiced threats to education workers if they continued the strike. Schools in all counties nevertheless remained shut down. Having failed to reopen schools singlehandedly, Justice turned to

> union leadership from WVEA and AFT-WV [who] announced that they arranged with Governor Justice a tentative deal

> to increase public employee pay by five percent alongside a sixteen-month freeze on insurance premiums. The PEIA task force that Justice said he was keen on creating would be developed a few weeks later. Flanked by state leadership from the main education unions, Justice stated that this deal was contingent upon teachers returning to work after a "cooling off" day on Wednesday. "The long and the short of it is just this: We need our kids back in school," Justice said. "We need our teachers back in school. They want to be back in school."[25]

In defiance of both the governor and union leaders, the intended two-day strike "ended up lasting thirteen days, resulting in a 5 percent raise for all employees, a 'freeze' on changes to PEIA, a task force appointed to fix PEIA, and the elimination of bills that would have further hurt education in West Virginia (charter schools, ending seniority, etc.). United, public employees had forced their legislature to listen."[26] The success of the worker-led 2018 strike can be attributed to several factors. It was led by the rank and file, to be sure, but it was also occasioned by a strong degree of solidarity that cut across the boundaries of the three unions. It was the first education strike in West Virginia that included all sectors of public school staff and was by no means limited to teachers. This meant, in contrast to the 1990 strike, that county school superintendents might issue announcements that schools would be open, but such proclamations were meaningless when no buses would run.

The rank-and-file movement that pulled off the 2018 school strike was horizontally organized and led, reflecting a historical model that had more in common with the revolutionary syndicalism of the early decades of the twentieth century than the prevailing regime that has come to predominate organized labor in the US since the Wagner Act of 1935.[27] On Tuesday, February 27, after four days of striking, there was a press conference with Justice, flanked by the leaders of WVEA and AFT-WV, to announce reaching a deal to end the walkout. The plan provided for February

28 to be a "cooling-off period," after which all schools would reopen. Nevertheless, thousands of public school workers chanting, "We won't back down," gathered at the state capitol, signaling a rejection of the agreement as school workers in county after county met and resolved to continue the strike. Another mass rally was scheduled amid debate over whether the strikers should stage an occupation of the Capitol building.[28]

"We do not wish for rank-and-file to leave their primary unions," Muckian-Bates recalled in a talk on April 4, 2018, at a Labor Notes Conference, "but rather to engage in more direct efforts to hold their leadership accountable and ensure that whatever deals are made are done so with the full knowledge by all those involved." The Facebook-based insurgents had discovered that school employees, regardless of their formal union membership, shared "a common theme": "we're all pissed off at our union establishment, we're all pissed off at our legislature."[29] The defiance by school employees resonated with the general public and the strikers clearly were able to generate immense community support. The solidarity between strikers and the public was mutual, and in various counties, school employees, keenly aware that many students depended on school lunch programs for basic nutrition, organized the daily preparation and school bus route delivery of meals during the strike. This mutual aid was widely reciprocated as parents and supporters delivered food to the picket lines statewide. The public sympathy for West Virginia educational workers extended beyond the state line as the 2018 strike inspired school employees in Oklahoma, Arizona, and Kentucky to stage their own walkouts.[30]

2019 School Strike

Early in the 2019 regular legislative session, a bill to privatize public education through charter schools and vouchers for private schools titled as Senate Bill 451 was quickly moved through the state senate. In anticipation of its passage the newly formed West Virginia United Caucus, the organizational offspring of the Facebook group that pulled off the 2018 strike, began its resistance to the bill by staging school walk-in protests in twenty counties.[31] Once the bill cleared the House of Delegates, the three school unions called a strike on the evening of February 19, which closed schools in all but one county in West Virginia. The resulting two-day strike effectively caused the legislature to indefinitely postpone consideration of the bill for the duration of the regular session.[32] Undeterred, one of the privatization measures—legalizing charter schools—was revived by the legislature during a special session convened during the summer when schools were out as part of a successfully passed education omnibus bill.[33]

On its website, West Virginia United sought to draw the lessons of the preceding events under a statement of the new organization's "five principles." One principle identified was that of worker empowerment, that the members of the three educational unions could collectively wage struggles capable of winning demands. The second principle articulated was solidarity unionism, that the rank-and-file of the three unions had more in common than their separate organizational affiliations. The third principle addressed the neoliberal fiscal austerity brought on by regressive taxation with a call for the taxation of wealth. The fourth principle was a demand for social justice unionism that encompassed community and environmental causes beyond the workplace. The fifth principle invoked an expansion of participatory democracy reminiscent of the "Port Huron Statement" of SDS.[34]

CHAPTER 7

Conclusion

The American labor-management regime that arose in the New Deal, based upon the mechanisms of majority certification, exclusive representation, and collective bargaining was historically accompanied, and supplemented, by various programs for public assistance, all of which have served to mitigate class conflict and left capitalist social relations intact. The New Deal reforms peaked in the 1960s. Beginning in the 1970s, fiscal public policy began to shift toward a neoliberal state agenda that included a decline in unionization.[1]

At the outset of the 1970s, however, there existed many reasons to envision an alternate trajectory ahead. The significant growth of public sector unionization nationally—evident at local, state, and federal levels of government—gave rise to an expectation that some version of collective bargaining would eventually come to exist in West Virginia's public sector and that unions like the American Federation of State, County and Municipal Employees (AFSCME) and the Service Employees International Union (SEIU) would eventually rival the United Mine Workers of America (UMWA) in size and influence in the labor history of West Virginia. The ascendancy of neoliberalism, however, continually deferred if not permanently foreclosed that scenario. The combination of fiscal austerity in public expenditures that lessened social inequities, privatization of the public sector, and increasingly regressive tax policies, all exacerbated by deindustrialization through national trade policies, reinstituted the pattern of the extraction of the region's wealth that had dominated the history of the nineteenth and early twentieth centuries. Although this forestalled the expectation of a continued growth in union organization in the state's public sector, it also had the effect of intensifying resistance by public workers, for example, displacing the likelihood of wildcat strikes erupting in traditional industries only to see them break out in public institutions.

Nevertheless, as historian Lou Martin has observed, despite all its ideological appeals to the "free market," the neoliberal agenda "is just as state-imposed as other economic systems."[2] This is amply illustrated in recent legislation. In 2016, the state lawmakers enacted an antiunion "right-to-work" law, bringing West Virginia's private sector employees into line with the Taft-Hartley provisions that had muted the Wagner Act provisions of the New Deal.[3] Under Senate Bill 1 of the 2016 legislative session, the state legislature enacted a law that not only prohibited a union security workplace wherein all employees of the certified private sector bargaining unit were required to be dues-paying members of the union, it also banned the use of agency fees to offset the costs of representing nonmembers.[4] In June 27, 2016, a number of unions filed a challenge to the Taft-Hartley "right-to-work" law, titled by its proponents in the Republican-dominated state legislature as the Workplace Freedom Act. On February 24, 2017, a preliminary injunction staying the enactment of the new law was granted in Kanawha County Circuit Court, based on presumptive grounds of its unconstitutionality. This injunction was in turn challenged by the state's attorney general, and on September 15, 2017, the state supreme court lifted the injunction and remanded the union's case to the circuit court.[5] On February 27, 2019, the circuit court issued a partial summary judgment finding that prohibiting agency fees while requiring the duly certified union to provide representation to nonmembers infringed upon state constitutional rights of association, property, and liberty. On March 27, 2019, the state attorney general again filed an appeal to the state supreme court, and in the following year, the latter reversed the summary judgment and declared the "right-to-work" law constitutional.[6] It was during this extended litigation over the fate of private sector union law in West Virginia that the 2018 and 2019 public school strikes occurred.[7] Rather than the expectation from a half-century before that union collective bargaining would eventually expand from the private sector to cover the public sector, the reverse occurred and existing union protections were significantly eroded in West Virginia's private sector.

Formed out of the public education workers Facebook group, the West Virginia United Caucus ran candidates for office in the West Virginia Education Association (WVEA), utilizing the five principles as well as a reform platform.[8] The West Virginia United slate included participants from the 2018 insurgency: Jay O'Neal for state president, Nichole McCormick for vice-president, and Jenny Craig, Leslie Haynes, and Daniel Hodges for executive committee positions. While they failed to unseat longstanding incumbents, the union's old guard faced the first significant challenge it had ever met, with president Dale Lee retaining his position with 60 percent of the vote.[9]

In 2021, a previously abandoned provision from legislation was revived that declared public school strikes illegal. Even with a Republican majority of 77 to 23, the House of Delegates barely mustered enough votes to pass the law, 53 to 46 delegates. As one Democratic delegate, Ed Evans of McDowell County, a school worker who had been in the 1990 strike, said at the time, if things were bad enough, school employees would strike whether it was legal or not.[10]

In what was universally regarded as retaliation for the public education strikes of 2018–19, in 2021 the West Virginia legislature enacted a Paycheck Protection Act, which prohibited the long-standing right of public employees to have union dues voluntarily deducted from their regular pay and remitted to their chosen organization, if any. Several unions challenged this provision and were granted a preliminary injunction by a Kanawha County circuit court judge. On November 21, 2021, the state supreme court, in a clear signal that it would uphold the act on eventual appeal, overturned the injunction.[11] Public sector unions, newly obliged to develop measures to collect dues from members, predictably suffered staggering losses until such measures could be devised and put in place.

One of the hardest hit by the new prohibition was the West Virginia Public Workers Union (WVPWU), which immediately lost more than three-quarters of its dues-paying membership when the provision went into effect in 2022. In the resulting turmoil, the national office of United Electrical, Radio and Machine Workers of America (UE) withdrew its single remaining staff member from West Virginia. Local 170 subsequently changed its elected leadership and went independent from UE on August 30, 2023, the day after UE removed its last staff member assigned to the state. In November 2024, WVPWU began implementing an approved proposal urging its membership, and public sector workers throughout the state, to join the UMWA's recently formed West Virginia state employee Local 154. Other unions also took various measures to recover membership losses. The West Virginia School Service Personnel Association (WVSSPA) affiliated with the UMWA in the summer of 2022. Following long-running rumors, it was announced in early 2024 that WVEA and the American Federation of Teachers-West Virginia (AFT-WV) were moving toward an eventual merger to be finalized in the following year.[12] Ironically, it took an attack by a hostile legislature to overcome the division that had been decried by rank-and-file dissidents at the inception of the 2018 strike movement.

In 2023, the legislature went after the admittedly already weak grievance procedure available to West Virginia's public workers. Revisions to the law went into effect in the summer of that year, the most far-reaching of which was to limit an employee's ability to represent fellow employees in more than five grievances in a one-year period, a restriction clearly aimed at shop stewards. That measure, along with incremental attacks on existing civil service protections, pointed to the weakened position of traditional public employee organizations in the state.

Overall, however, the legislative and neoliberal assaults on public sector union organizing that have been undertaken, particularly in the wake of the 2018–19 school strikes, may well prove to have been misplaced efforts on the part of the antilabor political regime exemplified in the likes of state senator Patricia Rucker and attorney general Patrick Morrisey. The focus on traditional labor unions with entrenched vertical bureaucracies and commitment to the conventional and continually deferred model of US collective bargaining may do little to suppress the possibility of public worker insurgency. They may do well to heed the observation, previously cited by a legislator, that illegality is no guarantee that there will never be strikes again.

The resilience of worker resistance is also suggested by historical experience, as shown in one analogy from even before the starting point of the instant narrative of public worker organizing in the 1969 West Virginia state road strike. In May 1968, millions of workers and students staged a general strike in France that nearly toppled the prevailing regime, and most certainly ushered in numerous social reforms in that country that reverberated on a global scale. That general strike wave erupted without the agency of traditional political parties, including those of the left, and without the leadership of the traditional unions.

After the enactment of the Wagner Act (1935), private sector collective bargaining in the US took the form of exclusive representation in a defined work unit for the negotiation of a contract once the union won a majority of votes in a certification election. In 1947, a number of practices by workers were curtailed with the passage of Taft-Hartley, which made sympathy strikes, boycotts, and wildcat strikes illegal, and allowed states to enact "right-to-work" provisions prohibiting closed shops. Public sector workers were not covered under Wagner, and as state legislatures began to extend collective bargaining to public employees, it was generally along the lines that had developed in the private sector, although often with an explicit ban on strikes.[13]

The history of public sector union organizing in West Virginia has been in many ways distinctive. As long as the UMWA remained a prominent force in West Virginia's private sector after the enactment of Wagner, the state, unlike other states of the southern US, was spared the open shop provisions of Taft-Hartley. For decades, therefore, West Virginia had one of the highest densities of unionization in its private sector. Throughout that time, however, West

Virginia made no provision for the unionization of government entities through legislation or through executive order. Although state and local public entities could enter into negotiated labor contracts, they were not obliged by law to do so, and the public sector remained largely unorganized.

In 2015, the Republican Party took control of the state legislature and passed Taft-Hartley-like provisions in 2016. After the sitting governor switched parties in 2018, Republican control of state government was solidified. The state federation of the AFL-CIO had throughout the latter half of the twentieth century exhibited only limited efforts at securing some form of public employee collective bargaining. Even those public entities with the greatest relative union density, the public schools, were the sites of a continual turf war between the independent staff union WVSSPA and conflicting state affiliates of the National Education Association (NEA) and the AFT. Apart from the brief period of the tentative merger between AFT-WV and WVSSPA and the more recent affiliation of WVSSPA with UMWA, only the smallest of the three unions, AFT-WV, was in the state federation.

The events of recent years have only rendered the prospect of the standard model of American public sector collective bargaining even more unlikely than ever in West Virginia. That said, the grassroots mobilization that erupted into the 2018 public school strike—with its spontaneous revival of workplace practices resembling those of revolutionary syndicalism—offers an alternative path to the long-elusive empowerment of public workers.

The strategy of the general strike has been present in American labor history since the 1877 upheaval that began in Martinsburg. It has also been a recurring theme in the revolutionary syndicalism that found expression in the Industrial Workers of the World, as well as in the working-class radicals during West Virginia's mine wars. The trajectory of public school strikes in this state alone—from 1980 to 1990 to 2018—and the national strike wave to which it gave rise suggest that the seemingly "inevitable" reign of neoliberalism may not prove to be the only arc of history available to the working people in public and private sectors alike.

Concluding Theses

1. In the modern social relation of wage labor, wherein the control of work is separated from the performance of work, workers have continually contested their subordination.
2. Strikes, including general strikes, have been a historical means by which wage workers contest that subordination, irrespective of whether strikes were legally sanctioned and whether the employer was a private capitalist or the state.
3. Unions in various formations historically emerged as means of worker self-organization.
4. Over time, unions frequently have assumed the form of ossified bureaucratic, vertical organizations, the activities and interests of which are capable of diverging to varying degrees from those of their members.
5. The presence of formal representational structures in any union is insufficient by itself to guarantee that such a union is a participatory democratic organization directed by its members, so that the struggle of workers against their condition of subordination frequently includes a struggle against bureaucratic union structures.
6. The New Deal labor relations regime and its public sector equivalences that allow some measure of legal union representation have historically abetted the tendency of recognized unions to assume ossified, bureaucratic organizational forms.
7. In a public sector where work stoppages and other forms of contestation are illegal, and where single or multiple unions may exist, workers can successfully self-organize by unofficial horizontal means in order to conduct extralegal activities necessary to contest their subordination.

Notes

Chapter 1: A Brief Labor History of West Virginia

1 Jeremy Brecher, *Strike!* (Straight Arrow Books, 1972), vii–viii.

2 D.C. Gallagher, "1876 Strike in Brownstown (Marmet)," *Charleston Gazette,* March 9, 1924.

3 Philip S. Foner, *The Great Labor Uprising of 1877* (Monad Press, 1977), 20.

4 Brecher, *Strike!*, 1–21.

5 Daniel Guerin, *100 Years of Labor in the USA* (Ink Links, 1979), 50–52.

6 Foner, *Great Labor Uprising*, 189.

7 Speech by J.P. McDonnell, quoted in Foner, *Great Labor Uprising*, 122.

8 Brecher, *Strike!*, 21.

9 Jean-Paul Sartre, *Critique of Dialectical Reason: Volume 1, Theory of Practical Ensembles* (New Left Books, 1976), 363ff.

10 Guerin, *100 Years*, 52.

11 There are numerous historical studies of Appalachian social, economic, and political development. One of the most recent and insightful is Steven Stoll, *Ramp Hollow: The Ordeal of Appalachia* (Hill and Wang, 2017).

12 On the role of the internal development of railroads in accelerating the wholesale destruction of the old-growth forest of Appalachia—a premonition of the late twentieth-century practice of coal strip-mining—see Ronald L. Lewis, *Transforming the Appalachian Countryside: Railroads, Deforestation, and Social Change in West Virginia, 1880–1900* (University of North Carolina Press, 1998). In timbering and the clear-cutting of West Virginia's forests, see also G.D. McNeill, *The Last Forest: Tales of the Allegheny Woods* (McClain Printing Company, 1940); and Roy B. Clarkson, *Tumult in the Mountains: Lumbering in West Virginia, 1770–1920* (McClain Printing Company, 1964).

13 The widespread adherence to unionist, cooperative, and socialist demands by immigrant glass workers in Appalachia was documented by Frederick A. Barker, *Cinderheads in the Hills; The Belgian Window Glass Workers in West Virginia* (West Virginia Humanities Council, 1988). The role of local elites, heavily invested in coal, to effect an "underdevelopment" of glass manufacturing was documented by Ken Fones-Wolf in "From Craft to Industrial Unionism in the Window Glass Industry: Clarksburg, West Virginia, 1900–1917," *Labor History* 37 (Winter 1995–96), and more explicitly in *Glass Towns: Industry, Labor, and Political Economy in Appalachia, 1890–1930s* (University of Illinois Press, 2007).

14 The thesis of "internal colonialism" is discussed in Helen Matthew Lewis, Linda Johnson, and Donald Adkins, eds., *Colonialism in Modern America: The Appalachian Case* (Appalachian Consortium Press, 1978). It should be noted that Fones-Wolf and some of the contributors to *Colonialism in Modern America* express reservations about applying the "colonialist" thesis to the Appalachian region. A detailed discussion of the acquisition of legal ownership, and the concurrent dispossession of residents, is found in Stoll, *Ramp Hollow*, 127ff.

15 Richard D, Lunt, *Law and Order vs. the Miners: West Virginia, 1907–1933* (Appalachian Editions, 1922). For the analysis of the national legal context for what happened in West Virginia, see Ahmed A. White, "The Crime of Industrial Radicalism: Criminal Syndicalist Laws and the Industrial Workers of the World, 1917–1927," *Oregon Law Review* 85, no. 649 (2006): 649–769; and Jim Pope, "Labor's Constitution of Freedom," *Yale Law Review* 106, no. 94 (1997): 941–1031.

16 The single best treatment and overview of this struggle is in David Alan Corbin, *Life, Work, and Rebellion in the Coal Fields: The Southern West Virginia Miners, 1880–1922* (University of Illinois Press, 1981).

17 David A. Corbin, "Betrayal in the West Virginia Coal Fields: Eugene V. Debs and the Socialist Party of America, 1912–1914," *Journal of American History* 64, no. 4 (March 1978): 987–1009. For a general history of the 1912–13 strike, see Lon Kelly Savage and Ginny Savage Ayers, *Never Justice, Never Peace: Mother Jones and the Miner Rebellion at Paint and Cabin Creeks* (West Virginia University Press, 2018). For the context of conflicting tendencies of moderates and revolutionaries within the Socialist Party, see Frederick A. Barkey, *Working Class Radicals: The Socialist Party in West Virginia, 1898–1920* (West Virginia University Press, 2012).

18 Corbin, *Life, Work, and Rebellion*, 97–100.

19 Corbin, *Life, Work, and Rebellion*, 87ff.

20 Corbin, *Life, Work, and Rebellion*, 210.

21 Corbin, *Life, Work, and Rebellion*, 100, 196.

22 Lon Savage, *Thunder in the Mountains: The West Virginia Mine War, 1920–21* (University of Pittsburgh Press, 1990), 19–24.

23 Corbin, *Life, Work, and Rebellion*, 215.

24 Corbin, *Life, Work, and Rebellion*, 210.

25 Savage, *Thunder in the Mountains*, 73.

26 Corbin, *Life, Work, and Rebellion*, 219.

27 Savage, *Thunder in the Mountains*, 148.

28 Keith Dix, *What's a Miner to Do? The Mechanization of Coal Mining* (University of Pittsburgh Press, 1988), 150ff.

29 For the contrast with working conditions before mechanization, see Carter Goodrich, *The Miner's Freedom* (Marshall Jones, 1925).

30 Dix, *What's a Miner to Do?*, 159–62.

31 Charles Keeney, "A Union Man: The Life of C. Frank Keeney, (master's thesis, Marshall University, 2000), 52–65. See also Gordon L Swartz, "West Virginia Mine Workers Union," in *The West Virginia Encyclopedia*, (West Virginia Humanities Council, 2006), 767.

32 Susan Kushner Resnick, *Goodbye Wifes and Daughters* (University of Nebraska Press, 2010), 39–44.

33 Paul Nyden, *Miners for Democracy: Struggle in the Coal Fields.* (Department of Sociology, University of Pittsburgh, 1974), 474.

34 Tony Boyle quoted in Ken Hechler, *The Fight for Coal Mine Health and Safety: A Documented History*, (Pictorial Histories Publishing Company, 2011), 75.

35 Bonnie E. Stewart, *No. 9: The 1968 Farmington Mine Disaster* (West Virginia University Press, 2011).

36 Kimberly Christensen, "'Dark as a Dungeon': Technological Change and Government Policy in the Deunionization of the American Coal Industry," *Review of Keynesian Economics* 2, no. 2 (Summer 2014): 160.

37 Alan Dericksen, "Down Solid: The Origins and Development of the Black Lung Insurgency," *Journal of Public Health Policy* 4, no. 1 (March 1983): 32–33.

38 Paul F. Clark, *The Miners' Fight for Democracy: Arnold Miller and the Reform of the United Mine Workers*, (Cornell University, 1981), 25.

39 Clark, *Miners' Fight for Democracy*, 26. An extensive account of Miners for Democracy can be found in Nyden, *Miners for Democracy*. For a concise treatment, see Christine M. Kreiser, "A Rumbling Down Below: Miners for Democracy," *Goldenseal* (Fall 2018): 58–67.

Chapter 2: 1969–1979

1 Evelyn L.K. Harris and Frank J. Krebs, *From Humble Beginnings: West Virginia State Federation of Labor, 1902–1957* (West Virginia Labor Federation Publishing Fund, 1960), 238, 456.

2 Harris and Krebs, *From Humble Beginnings*, 456.

3 Employees of the State Road Commission were at the time exempt from civil service coverage. Charles Matthew Kincaid, "Resolving Public Employment Disputes: A Guide for West Virginia," *West Virginia Law Review* 79, no. 1 (1976): 23.

4 These developments are extensively chronicled in Paul F. Clark, *The Miners' Fight for Democracy: Arnold Miller and the Reform of the United Mine Workers.* (New York State School of Industrial and Labor Relations, Cornell University, 1981); and Paul Nyden, "Miners for Democracy: Struggle in the Coal Fields" (PhD diss., Columbia University, 1974).

5 *Kirker v. Moore,* Memorandum Opinion, United States District Court, SD W.Va, Charleston Division, January 12, 1970, 308 F. Supp. 615.

6 *Kirker,* supra.

7 *Kirker,* supra.

8 *Kirker,* supra.

9 Leon Bornstein, "Developments in Industrial Relations," *Monthly Labor Review* 92, no. 96 (June 1969): 73.

10 The *Kirker* decision ultimately gave different numbers, based on a May 1, 1969, agency-provided analysis. In the *Kirker* decision, it was reported that 1,532 State Road Commission employees, including an unspecified total of rehired workers, remained employed, while 1,752 were discharged and not reemployed by the state.

11 *Kirker,* supra.

12 *Kirker,* supra.

13 *Kirker,* supra.

14 *Kirker,* supra, citing *City of Cleveland v. Division 268 Amalgamated Association*

of Street, Electric Railway and Motorcoach Employees of America, 90 N.E.2d 711 (Ohio Common Pleas 1949).

15 *Kirker,* supra.

16 See *Nunnery v. Barber,* 365 F. Supp. 691, 695 SD W.Va. 1973, *aff'd,* 503 F.2d 1349 (4th Cir. 1974), *cert. denied,* 420 US 1005 (1975), citing *AFSCME v. Shapp,* 443 Pa. 527, 536, 280 A.2d 375, 378 (1971).

17 The ongoing effects of, and challenges to, residual patronage are evident in several workplace grievances going back to the state's 1989 enactment of comprehensive civil service reform: *Lilly v. West Virginia Division of Highways,* Docket No. 07-DOH-387 (June 30, 2008); *Vance v. West Virginia Division of Highways,* Docket No. 06-DOH-418 (January 24, 2007); *Roush, et al. v. West Virginia Division of Highways,* Docket No. 01-DOH-573/561 (February 28, 2003); *Lowther v. West Virginia Division of Highways,* Docket No. 01-DOH-589); *Mercer v. West Virginia Division of Highways,* Docket No. 01-DOH-604 (March 20, 2002); *Blake v. West Virginia Division of Highways,* Docket No. 97-DOH-416 May 1, 1998). See also *Akers v. West Virginia Division of Highways,* 188 W.Va. 698, 425 S.E.2d 840 (1992); *Frantz, et al., v. West Virginia Department of Employment Services,* Docket No. 89-ES-050 (July 25, 1989).

18 *Mountaineer Public Employees Newsletter* 1, no. 4 (June 1972): 2.

19 Gergely Ujhelyi, "Civil Service Rule and Policy Choices: Evidence from US State Governments," *American Economic Journal: Economic Policy* 6, no. 2 (May 2014): 346–47.

20 John G. Morgan, "Better Civil Service Group's Top Aim," *Charleston Gazette,* October 4, 1972. The bills favored by WVPEA mirrored ones that had been introduced by Sen. William Brotherton.

21 Morgan, "Better Civil Service Group's Top Aim."

22 Morgan, "Better Civil Service Group's Top Aim."

23 *Mountaineer Public Employees Newsletter* 1, no. 4 (June 1972).

24 Hollie Brown, interview by author, September 10, 2023; and Kay Michael, "Public Employes' [*sic*] Strike Parallels First Walkout," *Charleston Gazette,* August 1, 1972.

25 Brown, interview, September 10, 2023; and Michael, "Public Employes'."

26 Joseph E. Slater, *Public Workers: Government Employee Unions, the Law, and the State, 1900–1962* (Cornell University Press, 2004), 164.

27 Slater, *Public Workers,* 164–65.

28 Len De Caux, *Labor Radical: From the Wobblies to CIO, A Personal History* (Beacon Press, 1970), 218.

29 Robert H. Ziegler, *The CIO: 1935–1955* (University of North Carolina Press, 1995), 29.

30 Ziegler, *CIO,* 31–41.

31 Slater, *Public Workers,* 126–27. Slater notes that UPWA attained a membership of more than a hundred thousand before its expulsion from the CIO in 1949 during the latter's anticommunist purge. Unlike the leftist public sector Transportation Workers Union, UPWA did not survive Cold War McCarthyism.

32 James O'Connor, *The Fiscal Crisis of the State* (St. Martin's Press, 1973), 238.

33 "We have termed this tendency for government expenditures to outrace revenues the 'fiscal crisis of the state.' There is no iron law that the

expenditures must always rise more rapidly than revenues, but it is a fact that growing needs which only the state can meet create ever greater claims on the state budget." O'Connor, *Fiscal Crisis*, 2.

34 O'Connor, *Fiscal Crisis*, 238–39. In terms that could equally apply to the public sector, O'Connor notes, "From the standpoint of monopoly capital the main function of unions was (and is) to inhibit disruptive, spontaneous rank-and-file activity (e.g. wildcat strikes and slowdowns) and to maintain labor discipline in general." O'Connor, *Fiscal Crisis*, 23.

35 O'Connor, *Fiscal Crisis*, 250.

36 William P. Jones, "The Road to Memphis: Southern Sanitation Workers and the Transformation of Public Employee Unionism in the Postwar United States," in *Public Workers in Service of America*, ed. Frederick W. Gooding Jr. and Eric S. Yellin (University of Illinois Press, 2023), 132–34.

37 Jones, "Road to Memphis," 138–42.

38 Joseph C. Goulden, *Jerry Wurf: Labor's Last Angry Man.* (Atheneum, 1982), 51–54; and Joseph E. Hower, "Jerry Wurf, the Rise of AFSCME, and the Fate of Labor Liberalism, 1947–1981" (PhD diss., Georgetown University, 2013), 21, 211. District Council 37 was cited by Robert Fitch as an example of an institutional capacity for corruption in his critique of the American style of collective bargaining. Fitch, *Solidarity for Sale: How Corruption Destroyed the Labor Movement and Undermined America's Promise* (Public Affairs, 2006), 162–88; see also Fitch, "Our Labor Leaders Need French Lessons," *New Politics* 1, no. 6 (Summer 1996).

39 "The growth of District Council 37 departed markedly from AFSCME's genteel brand of civil service unionism and its traditional base in rural, white-collar, and administrative sectors. Between 1961 and 1964, Wurf and his caucus, the Committee on Union Responsibility (COUR), evolved from reformist bloc to outright opposition, blending demands for a more confrontational and militant model of public sector unionism with indictments of the administration's handling of internal union democracy. Cobbling together a geographically and politically diverse slate of supporters, Wurf managed to successfully unseat Zander in 1964, a rare feat in national union elections in the postwar era." Hower, "Jerry Wurf," 22.

40 Jones, "Road to Memphis," 144.

41 Jones, "Road to Memphis," 136.

42 Hower, "Jerry Wurf," 19.

43 There are numerous accounts of the AFSCME Local 1733 strike in Memphis, especially Michael K. Honey, *Going Down Jericho Road: The Memphis Strike, Martin Luther King's Last Campaign* (W.W. Norton and Sons, 2008). See also, Hower, "Jerry Wurf," 245–56; and Goulden, *Jerry Wurf*, 142–82. A useful, if nonsouthern, precedent can also be found in Francis Ryan, "'They Won't Work for a Cop of Any Kind': The 1970 Sanitation Slowdown and the Struggle for Black Independent Politics in Philadelphia," in Gooding and Yellin, *Public Workers*, 149–74.

44 Kay Michael, "Public Employes' Strike Parallels First Walkout," *Charleston Gazette*, August 1, 1972.

45 Brown, interview, September 10, 2023. Describing his family's experience, Brown compared it to the actual historical character known as "Few Clothes" Johnson, played by James Earl Jones in John Sayles's movie *Matewan*.

46 Kay Michael, "Red Man Warrants Signed by Mayor in City Strike," *Charleston Gazette,* August 3, 1972. A half-century later, a Charleston journalist wrote about the incident: "Warrants were signed to charge Brown and other strikers with conspiracy for violating 'The Red Man Act,' an archaic piece of state code implemented in the 1800s to quell labor uprisings in the coalfields. Those charges against Brown were unfounded and eventually vacated, according to news reports. In 1975, a judge ruled the Red Man Act unconstitutional. The language remains on the state's books." Caity Coyne, "'We Wanted to See Real Change,' 50 Years After Charleston City Worker Strike," *Charleston Gazette-Mail,* November 5, 2022. It was so called because of the common designation of *West Virginia Code* §61-6-7 as the "Red Men Act," a conspiracy statute originally adopted in 1882 that began with a specific reference to the "Red Men." See *State v. Porter,* 25 W.Va. 685 (1885). It was invoked previously, for example, in a labor dispute after a picket of more than a hundred striking miners in Pocahontas County (appropriately enough) on September 10, 1954, sought to prevent a mine superintendent from entering the worksite by temporarily lifting the rear of his Buick. *State v. Winkler,* 95 S.E.2d 57 (1956). It was eventually declared to be an unconstitutional denial of due process in *Pinkerton v. Farr,* 159 W.Va. 223 (1975). Hutchinson's use of the Red Men Act also resonated with the early existence of a "criminal syndicalism" law in West Virginia in 1919 aimed at making membership in the Industrial Workers of the World illegal. See Ahmed A. White, "The Crime of Economic Radicalism: Criminal Syndicalist Laws and the Industrial Workers of the World, 1917–1927," *Oregon Law Review* 85, no. 649 (2006). Frederick Barkey, the leading historian of early coalfield political radicalism has drawn attention to the use of "fraternal" organizations like the Improved Order of Red Men as a cover for worker organizing and mutual aid in the early coalfields. Fred Barkey, "Red Men and Rednecks in the Fraternal Lodge in the Coal Fields," *West Virginia Historical Quarterly* 17, no. 1 (January 2003).

47 Kay Michael, "Permanent Injunction to Be Pressed by City," *Charleston Gazette,* August 5, 1972.

48 Kay Michael, "Workers Given Last Chance for Jobs," *Charleston Gazette,* August 8, 1972.

49 Kay Michael, "48 City Workers Fired, Others Offered Old Jobs," *Charleston Gazette,* August 9, 1972. Brown recalls that his attorney quickly sprung him on the public intoxication charge and they went to Charleston General Hospital, where he tested as having no alcohol in his system and was treated for being injured when police slammed his foot in the door of the paddy wagon. Brown, interview by author, October 1, 2023.

50 Coyne, "'We Wanted to See Real Change.'"

51 Thomas Knight, "Must Uphold the Law, Mayor Says," *Charleston Gazette,* September 19, 1972.

52 Kay Michael, "Abernathy to Lead March of City Strikers Monday," *Charleston Gazette,* September 25, 1972.

53 Kay Michael, "Abernathy Vows to Return if the Strike Not Settled," *Charleston Gazette,* September 26, 1972.

54 Kay Michael, "Strike Illegal, Stop Picketing, Judge Decrees," *Charleston Gazette,* September 28, 1972.

55 Goulden, *Jerry Wurf*, 160.

56 Kay Michael, "City Picket Lines Fall, But Strikers Won't Quit," *Charleston Gazette*, September 29, 1972.

57 Kay Michael, "City Won't Hire Back 'Fired 52,'" *Charleston Gazette*, October 3, 1972.

58 Michael, "City Won't Hire Back 'Fired 52.'"

59 The Civil Service Commission had an appeal pending before the state supreme court on the case of former city employee H.L. "Bus" Jarrell. Jarrell's case had already gone through Kanawha County Court of Pleas and Kanawha County Circuit Court before being appealed to the state supreme court. A former assistant collector for the city, Jarrell had asked for back pay for the period before his firing in June 1971, and involved "a testing of the validity of the Civil Service Commission." Kay Michael, "Mayor, Councilman Swap Confirmed," *Charleston Gazette*, October 3, 1972.

60 Michael, "Mayor, Councilman Swap Confirmed."

61 Thomas Gagliardo, interview, *Charleston Gazette*, October 6, 1972.

62 Gagliardo, interview.

63 Gagliardo, interview.

64 Kay Michael, "Jail or Jobs, Marchers Say," *Charleston Gazette*, October 13, 1972.

65 Kay Michael, "No Jail for Protesters," *Charleston Gazette*, October 14, 1972.

66 Nyden, "Miners for Democracy," 878.

67 Hollie Brown, interview by author, October 1, 2023.

68 For the history of Local 1199, see Leon Fink and Brian Greenberg, *Upheaval in the Quiet Zone: A History of Hospital Workers' Union Local 1199* (University of Illinois Press, 1989).

69 Woodruff, along with Danie Stewart and other students at Huntington's Marshall University founded a campus chapter of the Students for a Democratic Society (SDS) in 1968, on the heels of a previous attempt in 1965. John Hennen, "Struggle for Recognition: The Marshall University Students for a Democratic Society and the Red Scare in Huntington, 1965–1969," *West Virginia History* 52 (1993): 127–47. The original draft of SDS's *Port Huron Statement*, a call for participatory democracy, contained a pointed critique of the hierarchical, business unionism that defined the AFL-CIO. In 1969, Woodruff, Stewart, and others also founded Appalachian Movement Press, a New Left publisher. Shaun Slifer, "So Much to Be Angry About: Appalachian Movement Press 1969–1979," *Signal: A Journal of International Political Graphics and Culture* (PM Press, 2018), 132–73.

70 John Hennen, *A Union for Appalachian Healthcare Workers: The Radical Roots and Hard Fights of Local 1199* (West Virginia University Press, 2021), 95–103.

71 *City of Fairmont v. Retail, Wholesale, & Department Store Union,*166 W.Va. 283 S.E.2d 589 (1980).

72 *City of Fairmont,* supra.

73 *City of Fairmont,* supra.

74 *City of Fairmont,* supra.

75 Justice Darrell McGraw quoting a 1969 ruling, *AFSCME, AFL-CIO v. Woodward,* 406 F.2d 137, 139 (8th Cir. 1969).

76 *City of Fairmont,* supra.

77 *City of Fairmont,* supra. It is worth noting that Local 1199 signed its first contract with Fairmont General in 1979, one year before the issuance of the

court's decision articulating the right to organize the facility. The union's representation of Fairmont General employees was to continue well after the hospital was changed from a municipal entity to a private, nonprofit facility, confirming McGraw's observation. Hennen, *Union for Appalachian Healthcare Workers*, 175.

78 Hennen, *Union for Appalachian Healthcare Workers*, 140.

79 Hennen, *Union for Appalachian Healthcare Workers*, 141–46.

80 Hennen, *Union for Appalachian Healthcare Workers*, 147.

81 Cal Winslow, "Overview: The Rebellion from Below, 1965–81," in *Rebel Rank and File: Labor Militancy and Revolt from Below in the Long 1970s*, ed. Aaron Brenner, Robert Brenner, and Cal Winslow (Verso, 2010), 6–7.

82 Paul Nyden, "Rank and File Movements in the United Mine Workers of America, Early 1960s–Early 1970s," in Brenner, Brenner, and Winslow, *Rebel Rank and File*, 186–87. Miller's reelection in 1977 as union president was accomplished by a plurality of less than 40 percent in a three-candidate race. Nyden, "Rank and File Movements," 188.

83 Nyden, "Rank and File Movements," 190.

84 Nyden, "Rank and File Movements," 194–96. For a concise analysis of the strike, see James Green, "Holding the Line: Miners' Militancy and the Strike of 1978," in *Workers' Struggles: Past and Present: A "Radical America" Reader* (Temple University Press, 1983), 321–43. Contemporaneous accounts of the 1977–78 contract strike include Kim Moody and Jim Woodward, *Battle Line: The Coal Strike of '78* (Sun Press, 1978); Linda Nyden and Paul Nyden, "Showdown in Coal: The Struggle for Rank-and-File Unionism," *Miner's Report*, January 1978.

85 The persistence of wildcat strikes in the wake of the 1974 contract has been analyzed in terms of workers' autonomy by William Cleaver in "Wildcats in the Appalachian Coal Fields," in *Midnight Oil: Work, Energy, War, 1973–1992*, ed. Midnight Oil Collective (Autonomedia, 1992), 169–83.

86 Paul Nyden, "Rank-and-File Organizations in the United Mine Workers," *Insurgent Sociologist* 8, nos. 2–3 (Fall 1978): 30.

87 Mike Ely, "Miners Right to Strike Committee," *Against the Current*, March–April 2022, https://againstthecurrent.org/atc217/miners-right-to-strike-committee; and "Ambush at Keystone No. 1: Inside the Coal Miners' Great Gas Protest of 1974," Kasama Project, July 2009, https://www.socialisthistory.ca/PDF/Kasama/ambush_at_keystone_coal_miners_protest_kasama_pamphlet.pdf. This strategic employment was illustrated in "Strike Bulletin #3: Stop the Injunctions—Defend the Right to Strike," circulated by the Miners' Right-to-Strike Committee and the Miners' Committee to Defend the Right-to-Strike of Madison and Beckley, WV, respectively.

88 A. Belden Fields, *Trotskyism and Maoism: Theory and Practice in France and the United States* (Autonomedia, 1988); Max Elbaum, *Revolution in the Air: Sixties Radicals Turn to Lenin, Mao and Che* (Verso, 2018); and Aaron J. Leonard and Conor A. Gallagher, *Heavy Radicals: The FBI's Secret War on America's Maoists, The Revolutionary Union/ Revolutionary Communist Party 1968–1980* (Zero Books, 2014); and Aaron J. Leonard and Conor A. Gallagher, *A Threat of the First Magnitude: FBI Counterintelligence and Infiltration from the Communist Party to the Revolutionary Union—1962–1974* (Repeater Books, 2017).

89 Charles M. Kincaid, "Resolving Public Employment Disputes: A Guide for West Virginia," *West Virginia Law Review* 79, no. 1 (1976): 23, 25. Kincaid was able to base this observation on the 1972 Census of Governments, a source for the percentage of state government unionization.

Chapter 3: The 1980s

1 Betsy Cook, "Teachers in 30 Counties Vote to Walk Out," *Charleston Gazette,* March 21, 1980.

2 Mark Ward, "Thousand Rally to Push Pay Hike," *Charleston Gazette,* March 22, 1980.

3 Marjorie Murphy, *Blackboard Unions: The AFT and the NEA, 1900–1980* (Cornell University Press, 1990).

4 Murphy, *Black Board Unions,* 3.

5 All of these distinctions and their evolution over time are thoroughly treated by Marjorie Murphy in *Blackboard Unions,* and "Militancy in Many Forms: Teachers Strikes and Urban Insurrection, 1967–74," in *Rebel Rank and File: Labor Militancy and Revolt from Below During the Long 1970s,* ed. Aaron Brenner, Robert Brenner, and Cal Winslow (Verso, 2010), 229–48.

6 Murphy, *Black Board Unions,* 272.

7 Ancella Bickley, *History of the West Virginia State Teachers' Association* (National Educational Association, 1979), 35.

8 Bickley, *History,* 38–39, 89.

9 Bickley, *History,* 92–94. It should be noted that for one of the underlying cases in *Brown,* prominent West Virginia lawyer and politician John W. Davis had argued in favor of preserving segregation. Gretchen Krantz-Evans in *The West Virginia Encyclopedia,* ed. Ken Sullivan (West Virginia Humanities Council, 2006), 186.

10 Bickley, *History,* 96–99.

11 Bickley, *History,* 104.

12 Cook, "Teachers in 30 Counties."

13 William Hal Gorby, "Balancing the Budget on the Back of Education: Neoliberalism and the 1990 West Virginia Teachers' Strike," *West Virginia History: A Journal of Regional Studies* 17, no. 1 (Spring 2023): 35.

14 *Pauley v. Kelly,* 162 W.Va. 672, 255 S.E.2d 859 (1979).

15 *Pauley v. Bailey,* 174 W. Va. 167, 324 S.E.2d 128 (1984). For a concise account of the public school funding controversy, see William McGinley, "Recht Decision," *West Virginia Encyclopedia* (West Virginia Humanities Council, 2006), 604.

16 Gorby, "Balancing the Budget," 36.

17 John Hennen, *A Union for Appalachian Healthcare Workers: The Radical Roots and Hard Fights of Local 1199* (West Virginia University Press, 2021), 168.

18 *Woodruff v. Board of Trustees of Cabell Huntington Hospital,* 173 W. Va. 604, 319 S.E.2d 372 (1984).

19 *Woodruff,* supra.

20 *Woodruff,* supra.

21 Among the federal decisions referenced by the state court were *Pickering v. Board of Education; Connick v. Myers; Branti v. Finkel; Perry v. Sindermann;* and *Keyishian v. Board of Regents. Woodruff,* supra.

22 *Woodruff*, supra, citing *Gooden v. Board of Appeals of the West Virginia Department of Public Safety* (1977).

23 *Woodruff*, supra.

24 Donna J. Walbrown, *Roane County Journal* 2, no. 2 (Winter 1994).

25 Hennen, *Union for Appalachian Healthcare Workers*, 187.

26 *AFSCME Local 586 v. City of Huntington*, 173 W.Va. 403 (1984).

27 *AFSCME Local 586*, supra.

28 *AFSCME Local 586*, supra.

29 *ATU Local Division 812 v. Central West Virginia Transit Authority*, 179 W.Va. 31 (1987).

30 *ATU Local Division 812*, supra.

31 *ATU Local Division 812*, supra.

32 Phil Edwards, *Status Report on Public Employee Organization in West Virginia* (Southern West Virginia Center for Labor Management Initiatives, 1992).

33 It was reported by Edwards that CWA was actively interested in organizing all employees in all areas of state government, with the largest agencies, including the AFSCME targets of DOH and DHHR, as priority recruiting projects. Phil Edwards, March 3, 1991, CWA survey.

34 *Annual Report to the Governor and the Legislature* (West Virginia Education and State Employees Board, 1998); Phil Edwards, *Status Report on Public Employee Organization in West Virginia* (West Virginia Labor Management Council, 1993). For educational administrator opposition to public collective bargaining, see Michael Wayne McPherson, "Study of the Attitude of Educational Leaders in West Virginia Toward Collective Bargaining and Selected Demographic Variables" (PhD diss., Virginia Polytechnic Institute and State University, July 1986). A former WVEA staff lawyer and former grievance administrative law judge asserts that the grievance procedure was a compromise measure for full-blown collective bargaining. William McGinley, interview by author, July 21, 2023.

35 *West Virginia Code* §18-29-1, *et seq.*, *West Virginia Code* §29-6A-1, *et seq.*

36 Weston State Hospital was later replaced by William R. Sharpe, Jr., Hospital, also in Weston, and Welch Emergency was renamed Welch General Hospital. Kim Jacks, "Weston State Hospital" (master's thesis, West Virginia University, 2008).

37 *District 1199 WV/KY/OH National Union of Hospital and Health Care Employees v. West Virginia Department of Health*, 180 W.Va. 506 (1989).

38 Quoted in W. Clayton Burch, *West Virginia School Laws Annotated* (LexusNexus, 2020), 823.

39 The dialectical intersection between cultural and class conflicts has been abundantly explored; to mention but two examples, see Dick Hebdige, *Subculture: The Meaning of Style* (Routledge, 1979), and Greil Marcus, *Lipstick Traces: A Secret History of the Twentieth Century* (Harvard University Press, 1989).

40 *Webb v. Mason County Board of Education*, Docket No. 26-88-206 (January 5, 1989).

41 Kanawha County Civil Action No. 89-AA-29.

42 *Webb v. Mason County Board of Education*, Docket No. 26-89-004 (May 1, 1989); Kanawha Co *Webb v. Mason County Board of Education*, Docket No. 89-26-56 (November 29, 1989).

43 Kanawha County Civil Action No. 89-AA-107 (October 24, 1989).

Chapter 4: The 1990s

1 Michael Mochaidean, "The Other West Virginia Teachers Strike," *Jacobin*, April 9, 2018, https://jacobin.com/2018/04/west-virginia-teachers-strike-1990-unions, points out the influence of the UMWA walkout on teachers. On the Pittston strike generally, see Richard A. Brisbin Jr., *A Strike Like No Other Strike: Law and Resistance during the Pittston Coal Strike of 1989–1990* (West Virginia University Press, 2010); and Richard A. Couto, "The Memories of Miners and the Conscience of Capital: Coal Miners' Strikes as Free Spaces," in *Fighting Back in Appalachia: Traditions of Resistance and Change*, ed. Stephen L. Fisher (Temple University Press, 1993), 165–94. William Hal Gorby also notes the influence of the UMWA strike against A.T. Massey as an influence on WVEA rank and file, William Hal Gorby, "Balancing the Budget on the Back of Education: Neoliberalism and the 1990 West Virginia Teachers' Strike," *West Virginia History: A Journal of Regional Studies* 17, no. 1 (Spring 2023): 39–40.

2 Gorby, "Balancing the Budget," 36.

3 Gorby, "Balancing the Budget," 38.

4 William McGinley, interview by author, July 21, 2023.

5 Gorby, "Balancing the Budget," 42–44.

6 Gorby, "Balancing the Budget," 42–44.

7 Marjorie Murphy, *Blackboard Unions: The AFT and the NEA, 1900–1980* (Cornell University Press, 1990), 227–29, 249; Phil Edwards, *Status Report on Public Employee Organization in West Virginia* (Southern West Virginia Center for Labor Management Initiatives, 1992).

8 Gorby, "Balancing the Budget," 42–44.

9 Gorby, "Balancing the Budget," 45–46.

10 McGinley, interview; Edwards, *Status Report.*

11 Gorby, "Balancing the Budget," 46.

12 "Opinion of the Attorney General's Office Regarding Whether the Strike by West Virginia's Teachers Is Legal and What May Be Done If Not (March 8, 1990)," https://ago.wv.gov/publicresources/Documents/Opinions%20 1986-1994/1990-03-08%20Opinion%20letter%20signed%20by%20 Roger%20Tompkins%20(M0040939xCECC6).PDF.

13 *Jefferson County Board of Education v. Education Association*, 393 S.E.2d 653 (1990).

14 Edwards, *Status Report.*

15 Edwards, *Status Report.* The commission issued its *Report to the Governor of the Blue Ribbon Personnel Commission* on December 17, 1992.

16 "The rapid growth of collective bargaining in the public sector during the 1960's can be attributed in large part to President Kennedy's Executive Order 10988 in 1962." Michael Wayne McPherson, "Study of the Attitude of Educational Leaders in West Virginia Toward Collective Bargaining and Selected Demographic Variables" (PhD diss., Virginia Polytechnic Institute and State University, July 1986), 24. The use of an executive order instead of enabling legislation had one obvious drawback: The next governor could rescind it.

17 For an account of the rise and fall of Marland's career, see Paul Lutz, *From Governor to Cabby* (Marshall University Library, 1995).

18 Gorby, "Balancing the Budget," 32.

19 *Whipkey, et al. v. West Virginia University,* Docket No. 90-BOT-2016 (July 2, 1991). The grievance was eventually dismissed on grounds that AFSCME had no standing to contest the issue under the grievance law.

20 Edwards, *Status Report.*

21 *West Virginia Code* §18-11C, West Virginia University Hospital and West Virginia Health System (1984). "The creation of a nonstock, not-for-profit corporation to which West Virginia University Hospital medical center facilities would be transferred, and which would then finance the construction of a new medical center does not violate West Virginia Constitution Article XI §1 providing that corporations are to be created under general laws, or Article X §6, forbidding that the state grant credit to or become liable for the debts of any corporation." *Queen v. West Virginia University Hospital,* 179 W.Va. 95, 365 S.E.2d 378 (1987).

22 Lou Martin, "Appalachia in the Neoliberal Era," *West Virginia History: A Journal of Regional Studies* 17, no. 1 (Spring 2023): 15.

23 "The corporation may utilize both corporation employees and university personnel on or after the transfer date, each university employee working in the hospital shall elect to be either a corporation employee or a part of university personnel. No university employee may be required to become an employee of the corporation as the condition of employment or promotion. All university personnel are university employees in all respects." *West Virginia Code* §18-11C-4(d).

24 *Prince v. West Virginia University,* Docket No. 92-BOT-365 (May 21, 1993).

25 *Seddon v. Kanawha-Charleston Health Department,* Docket No. 90-H-115 (June 8, 1990).

26 *Chafin v. Boone County Health Department,* Docket No. 92-HHR-132 (July 24, 1992); and Boone County Civil Action #92-C-342 (November 24, 1993).

27 *Chafin v. Boone County Board of Health,* 192 W.Va. 202, 451 S.E.2d 768 (1994).

28 *Graley v. West Virginia Parkways Economic Development and Tourism Authority,* Docket No. 91-PEDTA-225 (December 23, 1991).

29 *Kirkpatrick v. Mid-Ohio Valley Transit Authority,* 188 W.Va. 247, 423 E.E.2d 856 (1992).

30 *Kirkpatrick,* supra.

31 *Bryant, et al., v. Logan County Board of Education,* Docket No. 02-23-047 (November 21, 2002).

32 *Bryant,* supra.

33 McGinley, interview.

34 *West Virginia Code* §18A-4-8b(a) (1983) as interpreted by the state supreme court in Syllabus point 1, *Dillon v. Wyoming County Board of Education,*177 W.Va. 145, 351 S.E.2d 58 (1986).

35 *West Virginia Code* §18A-4-7a (1990).

36 Syllabus point 4, *Wood County Board of Education v. Enoch,* 186 W.Va. 712, 414 S.E.2d 630 (1992).

37 *Triggs v. Berkeley County Board of Education,* Docket No. 89-02-270 (April 30, 1990).

38 *Triggs v. Berkeley County Board of Education,* 425 E.E.2d 111 (W.Va. 1992).

39 *Chafin et al., v. Boone County Board of Education,* Docket No. 93-03-034 (July 7, 1993).

40 *Largent v. West Virginia Division of Health,* 452 S.E.2d 42 (November 18, 1994). When a former lawyer for WVEA later became a grievance board administrative law judge, he expressed some dismay that the supreme court in *Largent* had essentially gutted seniority considerations in pay issues for state agency employees. McGinley, interview.

Chapter 5: The 2000s

1 American Federation of State, County and Municipal Employees, "Constitution for Local 3248," March 26, 2001.

2 The antimony of low-density public employment organization in an otherwise highly unionized West Virginia did not go unnoticed. See Charles Matthew Kincaid, "Resolving Public Employee Disputes: A Guide for West Virginia," *West Virginia Law Review* 79 (1976).

3 Mary Ann Uzelac, "Public Employees Deserve Better," *Charleston Daily Mail,* May 23, 2001.

4 Uzelac, "Public Employees"; *Report to the Governor of the Blue Ribbon Personnel Commission.*

5 Uzelac, "Public Employees." Despite her labor bona fides, Uzelac's editorial was published in the *Charleston Daily Mail,* a bastion of conservative antiunion opinion. The Independent Union of Public Employees apparently was unable to gain any significant traction and faded into obscurity.

6 The emergence of staff unions within labor organizations has been a neglected area of study, perhaps because it rather effectively refutes the exclusivist canard of "dual unionism" as a cardinal sin within the US labor regime. The emergence of staff unions, even within more ostensibly radical labor organizations such as UE, indicates an unresolved contradiction inherent in all forms of vertical unionism. There has been some sympathetic treatment of staff unions in the radical press, see Guillermo Perez, "The Role of Staff Unions in the Labor Movement: Interview with Paul Krehbiel," *Labor Notes,* August 28, 2007, https://labornotes.org/2007/08/role-staff-unions-labor-movement-interview-paul-krehbiel; Ned Resnikoff, "When the Union's the Boss," *Jacobin,* April 21, 2013, https://jacobin.com/2013/04/when-the-unions-the-boss.

7 *American Federation of State, County and Municipal Employees, Council 77, AFL-CIO v. United Staff Union - West Virginia.* National Labor Relations Board, Region 9. Case 9-UC-472. August 21, 2002.

8 *American Federation of State, County and Municipal Employees, Council 77, AFL-CIO v. United Staff Union.*

9 *Rutherford v. West Virginia Bureau of Employment Programs,* Docket No. 03-BEP-040D (March 24, 2003).

10 *Hammond, et al., v. West Virginia Division of Highways,* Docket No. 05-DOH-336B (February 14, 2008). According to a former Council 77 staff member, Hartman suddenly halted further membership recruitment when he realized that passing a numerical threshold would require additional reporting to the International. Rich Patrick, interview by author, August 5, 2023.

11 *Hammond, et al., v. West Virginia Division of Highways*, 727 S.E.2d 652 (2012).

12 General Services and Corrections employees were already provided uniforms, as were workers for the Parkways Authority through a clothing and boot allowance.

13 The rumor that circulated among DHHR staff was that the imposition of a dress code banning blue denim came after some state hospital workers on break had the nerve to approach the governor and his wife at a public restaurant in order to express their dissatisfaction over working conditions.

14 *Lilly, et al., v. West Virginia Department of Health and Human Resources*, Docket No. 05-HHR-491 (April 27, 2006).

15 *Nestor v. West Virginia Department of Health and Human Resources*, Docket No. 05-HHR-424 (April 28, 2006). Agency counsel in *Nestor* was Landon Brown, who would soon become an administrative law judge for the grievance board and became noted among the board's administrative judges for having the highest rate for denying employee grievances.

16 *King, et al., v. Lewis County Board of Education*, Docket No. 2014-0456-CONS (August 26, 2015).

17 The name was inspired by labor history: in part, by AFSCME's old rival, the United Public Workers of America, which had been expelled from the CIO as Communist-led, and perhaps in great part by the West Virginia Mine Workers, founded by Frank Keeney and others who had opposed John L. Lewis's autocratic regime in the UMWA.

18 Saladin Muhammad, "Raleigh City Workers Exercise Power and Build Their Union" (Black Workers for Justice, Rocky Mount, 2006). Years later, UE's director of organizing admitted that the union's national office had at the time been opposed to the Raleigh sanitation strike.

19 Vanessa Tait, *Poor Workers' Unions: Rebuilding Labor from Below* (South End Press, 2005): 149–51.

20 Peter Gilmore, a former *UE News* editor, in his foreword to James Young, *Union Power: The United Electrical Workers in Erie, Pennsylvania* (Monthly Review Press, 2017), 8.

21 There was some tension between the UE national office and the West Virginians, as evident in one early incident: When a staffer warned Dotson that if sign-ups fell short, the national office would pull out, a nearby member who overheard the staffer turned to Dotson and said, "Bruce, we're going to do this thing with or without them," leaving the staffer visibly dismayed. Dotson later made no attempt to conceal his pleasure in recalling the incident.

22 *Proceedings of the 70th UE Convention*, Pittsburgh: September 16–20, 2007, 9, 185–86.

23 The core maintenance plan was eventually codified as written policy on July 15, 2010, as part of the agency's *Administrative Operating Procedures*, Section V, Chapter 15.

24 "Report of the West Virginia Legislative Auditor, Performance Evaluation and Research Division, January 2019, PE18-15-621."

25 Under the new regime, one county administrator was disciplined for having authorized a major paving project, despite any lack of specificity as to what constituted a "major" project under the new guidelines imposed by the

Manchin administration. *Lilly v. West Virginia Division of Highways,* Docket No. 07-DOH-387 (June 30, 2008).

26 Kate White, *Charleston Gazette,* March 7, 2014.

27 *Hur Herald,* September 15, 2007.

28 *Daily Kos,* August 24, 2007.

29 *Hur Herald,* September 15, 2007.

30 "Stop Privatization" flyer, WVPWU, August 25, 2007.

31 Paul Nyden, *Charleston Gazette,* February 24, 2008.

32 Nyden, *Charleston Gazette,* February 24, 2008.

33 *Roush v. West Virginia Division of Highways,* Docket No. 2008-0782-DOT (October 31, 2008).

34 *Roush v. West Virginia Division of Highways,* Civil Action No. 09-C-1670.

35 Alsop later, in 2023, acquired some infamy of his own as the hatchet man who eliminated faculty positions and academic disciplines at West Virginia University under the administration of WVU President Gordon Gee and Governor Jim Justice.

36 Minutes of the 2008 State Convention, West Virginia Public Workers Union, August 23, 2008.

37 Minutes of the WVPWU Executive Committee, June 9, 2009; July 2009 WVPWU newsletter.

38 Minutes of the WVPWU Executive Committee, June 9, 2009; July 2009 WVPWU newsletter.

39 Patrick Thibodeau, "West Virginia's IT Workers Fight State Outsourcing," *Computerworld,* September 1, 2010.

40 Minutes of the WVPWU Executive Committee, September 14, 2010.

41 Minutes of the WVPWU Executive Committee, September 14, 2010.

42 Minutes of the WVPWU Executive Committee, October 12, 2010.

43 Jennifer Ayers, email to Pam Schwarz and Steve Thompson, January 26, 2011, 11:17 pm.

44 Ayers, email.

45 Ayers, email.

46 Ayers, email.

47 Ayers, email.

48 Ayers, email.

49 *Goodman, et al., v. West Virginia Division of Highways,* Docket No. 2019-0863-CONS. On June 25, 2020, DOH submitted a seven-hundred-page proposed pay plan to SPB to fulfill the 2017 statutory mandate.

50 Eric Eyre, "WV DOH Spent $240K on 'Unnecessary' Comp Time Buyouts," *Charleston Gazette,* May 19, 2016.

51 Kate White, "Kanawha Teachers Protest Planned Clothing Rules," *Charleston Gazette,* March 7, 2014.

52 Eric Eyre, "DOH Workers Told They Can't Buy Surplus State Equipment," *Charleston Gazette,* August 13, 2014.

53 Eric Eyre, "Indicted Ex-DOH Official Commits Suicide, Police Say," *Charleston Gazette,* September 1, 2015.

54 Indictment, *United States v. Robert Glen Andrew, II, and MoTrim Incorporated,* United States District Court for the Northern District of West Virginia, September 1, 2015.

55 Eyre, "Indicted ex-DOH Official Commits Suicide."

56 *West Virginia Code* §18-29-1, *et seq.*

57 *West Virginia Code* §29-6A-1, *et seq.*

58 *West Virginia Code* §18-29-1 to 18-29-11 and *West Virginia Code* §29-6A-1 to 29-6A-12 were repealed and replaced by *West Virginia Code* §6C-2-1 to 6C-2-7 and *West Virginia Code* §6C-3-1 to 6C-3-6 (2007).

59 *West Virginia Code* §6C-2-2(n): "'Representative' means any employee organization, fellow employee, attorney or other person designated by the grievant or intervenor as his or her representative and may not include a supervisor who evaluates the grievant." §6C-2-3(g)(1): "An employee may designate a representative who may be present at any step of the procedure as well as at any meeting that is held with the employee for the purpose of discussing or considering disciplinary action."

60 *Swiger v. West Virginia Civil Service Commissioner*, 179 W.Va. 133, 365 S.E.2d 797 (1988).

61 "The Due Process Clause, Article III, Section 10 of the West Virginia Constitution, requires procedural safeguards against State action which affects a liberty or property interest." Syllabus point 1, *Waite v. Civil Service Commission*, 161 W.Va. 154, 241 S.E.2d 164 (1977), overruled in part on other grounds by *West Virginia Department of Education v. McGraw*, 239 W.Va. 192, 201, 800 S.E.2d 230, 239 (2017). "A State civil service classified employee has a property interest arising out of the statutory entitlement to continued uninterrupted employment." *Id.* at Syllabus point 4. "The constitutional guarantee of procedural due process requires 'some kind of hearing' prior to the discharge of an employee who has a constitutionally protected property interest in his employment." *Cleveland Board of Education v. Loudermill*, 470 U.S. 532, 542 [84 L. Ed. 2d 494, 105 S. Ct. 1487] (1985)." Syllabus point 3, *Fraley v. West Virginia Civil Service Commission*, 177 W.Va. 729, 356 S.E.2d 483 (1987). "The pretermination hearing does not need to be elaborate or constitute a full evidentiary hearing. The essential due process requirements, notice and an opportunity to respond, are met if the tenured civil service employee is given 'oral or written notice of the charges against him, an explanation of the employer's evidence, and an opportunity to present his side of the story' prior to termination." *Id.* at 732, 356 S.E.2d at 486.

62 For an extensive treatment of the issue of legal interpretation with respect to workers' rights, see Jim Pope, "Labor's Constitution of Freedom," *Yale Law Review* 106, no. 94 (1997): 941–1031.

63 *Knight v. West Virginia Department of Health and Human Resources*, Docket No. 2008-0981-DHHR (August 6, 2009).

64 *Knight*, supra.

65 *Koblinsky v. Putnam County Health Department*, Docket No. 2010-1306-COND (November 8, 2010).

66 The ruling in *Koblinsky* further cited *Hammer v. Greenbrier County Board of Education*, Docket No. 2008-0302-GreED (May 21, 2008) (citing: Syllabus point 7, *Waite v. West Virginia Civil Service Commission*, 161 W.Va. 154, 241 S.E.2d 164 (1977); *Clarke v. West Virginia Board of Regents*, 166 W.Va. 702, 279 S.E.2d 169, 175 (1981) and *Knauff v. Kanawha County Board of Education*, Docket No. 20-88-095 (January 10, 1989).

67 *Beaton, et al., v. West Virginia Department of Health and Human Resources*, Docket No. 2013-0496-CONS (December 20, 2013).

68 *Beaton*, supra.

69 *Deyerle v. West Virginia Department of Health and Human Resources*, Docket No. 2013-2231-CONS (July 15, 2014).

Chapter 6: The 2010s

1 The county health department's executive director was not only found to have illegally denied the employee representation and due process—in the previously cited *Koblinsky v. Putnam County Health Department*, Docket No. 2010-1306-CONS (November 8, 2010)—but also to have later discharged the same employee for the exercise of free speech, and compounded those acts by paying its outside counsel's hefty fees rather than the monthly rent for the department's facilities, effectively shutting down the agency. *Koblinsky v. Putnam County Health Department*, Docket No. 2011-1772-CONS (October 23, 2012).

2 Kate White, "State Bar Panel Told Lawyers Should Not Be Required in Hearings," *Charleston Gazette-Mail*, September 3, 2015.

3 *Riddle v. West Virginia Department of Health and Human Resources*, Docket No. 2018-2029-DHHR (October 24, 2018).

4 *Broyles v. West Virginia Department of Health and Human Resources*, Docket No. 2019-0565-DHHR (April 24, 2020).

5 Matles was a long-time UE director of organizing.

6 The role of shop stewards, not only as an expression of rank-and-file democracy, but also historically in workplace struggles such as the 1970s strike waves, has been detailed in Sheila Cohen, *Ramparts of Resistance: Why Workers Lost Their Power, and How to Get in Back* (Pluto Press, 2006).

7 West Virginia School Service Personnel Association, *Constitution*, adopted September 25, 1965, amended October 2018.

8 Phil Edwards, *Status Report on Public Employee Organization in West Virginia* (West Virginia Labor Management Council, 1992).

9 Ryan Quinn, "Teacher, School Service Personnel Unions Split," *Charleston Gazette*, March 31, 2016. When AFSCME Council 77 disbanded in West Virginia, its municipal locals were placed under AFSCME's Ohio council, and the state members placed with AFT-WV. After the break between AFT-WV and WVSSPA, those state employees successfully petitioned the school service personnel to affiliate with their association as a chapter. Joe White, interview by author, May 21, 2021.

10 On September 20, 2010, the West Virginia Public Employees Grievance Board also listed a few smaller organizations registered as having to represent public employees in grievances: the American Teachers Union, the United School Service Employees Association, and the West Virginia Professional Educators. Of those, only the last group was surveyed by Edwards in the *Status Report*, at which time WVPE claimed 420 members and declared its opposition to both collective bargaining and strikes.

11 Elizabeth Catte, Emily Hilliard, and Jessica Salfia, eds., *55 Strong: Inside the West Virginia Teachers' Strike* (Belt Publishing, 2018), 21. For a concise account of the 2018 strike, see Nicole McCormick, "Owning My Labor," in *Strike For the Common Good: Fighting for the Future of Public Education* (University of Michigan Press, 2020), 112–16.

12 Michael Mochaidean, "Reds in the Hills: An Anarcho-Syndicalist

Interpretation of the Contemporary West Virginia Teachers' Strike," Hampton Institute, February 27, 2018, https://www.hamptonthink.org/read/the-reds-in-the-hills-an-anarcho-syndicalist-interpretation-of-the-contemporary-west-virginia-teachers-strike. Mochaidean is a *nom de plume* for Brendan Muckian-Bates.

13 Eric Blanc, *Red State Revolt: The Teachers' Strikes and Working-Class Politics* (Verso, 2019), 121.

14 Lois Weiner, "Inside the Closed Facebook Groups Where Teacher Strikes Began," *In These Times,* May 18, 2018. Weiner's account makes insightful points about both the advantages and limitations of Facebook as an organizing tool for the rank and file.

15 Jane Slaughter, "West Virginia Teachers Learned from the 1970s Miners," *Labor Notes,* March 28, 2018, https://labornotes.org/blogs/2018/03/west-virginia-teachers-learned-1970s-miners..

16 See, for example, Jessica Salfia, introduction to *55 Strong,* 7; "Jay O'Neal," in *55 Strong,* 20; and Michael Mochaidean, "The Other West Virginia Teacher Strike," *Jacobin,* April 9, 2018, https://jacobin.com/2018/04/west-virginia-teachers-strike-1990-unions.

17 "Jay O'Neal," in *55 Strong,* 21.

18 Mochaidean, "Reds in the Hills."

19 Catte, Hilliard, and Salfia, *55 Strong,* 25.

20 Catte, Hilliard, and Salfia, *55 Strong,* 20.

21 Erin Dyke and Brendan Muckian-Bates. *Rank-and-File Rebels: Theories of Power and Change in the 2018 Education Strikes.* (University Press of Colorado, 2023), xi–xii.

22 Catte, Hilliard, and Salfia, *55 Strong,* 22.

23 Dyke and Muckian-Bates. *Rank-and-File Rebels,* xi.

24 Dyke and Muckian-Bates, *Rank-and-File Rebels,* xiii.

25 Dyke and Muckian-Bates, *Rank-and-File Rebels,* xiv–xv.

26 Catte, Hilliard, and Salfia, *55 Strong,* 22.

27 A detailed analysis of this feature is found in an essay by one of the original Facebook group participants in Michael Mochaidean, "Reds in the Hills: An Anarcho-Syndicalist Interpretation of the Contemporary West Virginia Teachers' Strike," Hampton Institute, February 27, 2018, https://www.hamptonthink.org/read/the-reds-in-the-hills-an-anarcho-syndicalist-interpretation-of-the-contemporary-west-virginia-teachers-strike. See also Michael Mochaidean, "The Teachers' Strike in West Virginia: Interview with IWW Teacher Michael Mochaidean," *It's Going Down,* March 12, 2018, https://itsgoingdown.org/teacher-strike-west-virginia-interview-iww-teacher-michael-mochaidean.

28 Michael Mochaidean, "How Teachers Resisted a Disappointing Deal," SocialistWorker.org, March 5, 2018, https://socialistworker.org/2018/03/05/how-teachers-resisted-a-disappointing-deal.

29 Michael Mochaidean, "Strike to Win: How the West Virginia Teacher Strike Was Won," Black Rose Anarchist Federation, April 10, 2018, https://www.blackrosefed.org/how-west-virginia-strike-won.

30 Erin Dyke and Brendan Muckian-Bates, "Educators Striking for a Better World: The Significance of Social Movement and Solidarity Unionisms," *Berkeley Review of Education* 9, no. 1 (2019).

31 Michael Mochaidean, "New Strike Possible as West Virginia Teachers Continue to Struggle," Black Rose Anarchist Federation, February 15, 2019, https://itsgoingdown.org/new-strike-possible-as-west-virginia-teachers-continue-struggle.
32 Associated Press, "Strike 2: West Virginia Teachers Walk Out in Protest," February 19, 2019, https://www.courthousenews.com/strike-2-west-virginia-teachers-walk-out-in-protest.
33 Ryan Quinn, "Lee Defeats O'Neal for WVEA Presidency; Other United Caucus Members Lose," *Charleston Gazette-Daily Mail,* January 17, 2020.
34 Brendan Muckian-Bates. "How We Organize to Win—Our Five Principles Explained," *West Virginia United,* accessed August 29, 2019.

Chapter 7: Conclusion

1 A recent summary of this shift and its implications for West Virginia can be found in Lou Martin, "Appalachia in the Neoliberal Era," *West Virginia History: A Journal of Regional Studies* 17, no. 1 (Spring 2023): 1–30.
2 Martin, "Appalachia in the Neoliberal Era," 7.
3 The American regime for private sector collective bargaining, known as the Wagner Act, was established in the wake of the 1935 National Labor Relations Act, and was diminished in 1947 with the Taft-Hartley Act, which allowed states to prohibit charging nonmembers union dues certified by the majority of employees in a collective bargaining unit. Those states were euphemistically termed "right-to-work" states. The union was, nevertheless, obligated to represent all employees including nonmembers. In states with public sector collective bargaining, this led to an arrangement whereby the union could charge a reduced agency fee to nonmembers, whom they were obligated to represent.
4 The legislated provisions became *West Virginia Code* §21-5G-1 *et seq.*
5 *Morrisey v. West Virginia AFL-CIO,* 804 S.E.2d 833 (2017), also known as *Morrisey 1.*
6 *Morrisey v. West Virginia AFL-CIO,* 842 S.E.2d 455 (2020), also known as *Morrisey 2.*
7 One concurring opinion in that decision observed that the intent of the law was to eliminate union power in line with the 2018 national judicial ruling in public sector law known as *Janus v. AFSCME,* and another opined that the solution to the dispute would henceforth be determined in the political rather than judicial realm. *Morrisey 2.*
8 Leslie Clayberger Haynes, "West Virginia Teachers Run for Top Union Offices," *Labor Notes,* May 5, 2020, https://labornotes.org/blogs/2020/05/west-virginia-teachers-run-top-union-offices.
9 Ryan Quinn, "Lee Defeats O'Neal for WVEA Presidency; Other United Caucus Members Lose," *Charleston Gazette-Daily Mail,* January 17, 2020. For examples of how a radicalizing caucus may be significant even when unsuccessful in winning internal union elections, see David Van Deusen, *Insurgent Labor: The Vermont AFL-CIO, 2017–2023.* (PM Press, 2024), 137–40.
10 Brad McElhinny, "House Narrowly Passes Bill Clarifying that Teacher Strikes Are Unlawful in West Virginia," *West Virginia Record,* March 2, 2021.
11 Kyla Asbury, "Supreme Court Reverses Decision Regarding New Paycheck Protection Law," *West Virginia Record,* December 14, 2021.

12 Carrie Hodousek, "WV Education Association, AFT-WV to Merge into One Organization," *West Virginia Metronews*, February 28, 2024, https://wvmetronews.com/2024/02/28/wv-education-association-aft-wv-to-merge-into-one-organization.

13 For one account of the May 1968 upheaval, see Daniel Cohn-Bendit and Gabriel Cohn-Bendit, *Obsolete Communism: The Left-Wing Alternative.* (McGraw-Hill, 1968).

Selected Bibliography

Ablavsky, Essie. "'This Is the Value of Our Labor': The Nonmajority Union Approach in U.S. Manufacturing." Undergraduate thesis, New College of Florida, 2012.

Alinsky, Saul. *John L. Lewis: An Unauthorized Biography*. G.P. Putnam's Sons, 1949.

Aronowitz, Stanley, and Jeremy Brecher. "Notes on the Postal Strike." *Root and Branch*, no. 1 (1970): 1–5.

Barkey, Frederick A., *Working Class Radicals: The Socialist Party in West Virginia, 1898–1920*. West Virginia University Press, 2012.

Befort, Stephen F. "The Constitutional Dimension of Unilateral Change in Public-Sector Collective Bargaining." *ABA Journal of Labor and Employment Law* 27, no. 2 (Winter 2012) 165–78.

Bethel, T.N. *Conspiracy in Coal*. Appalachian Movement Press, 1973.

Bickley, Ancella. *History of the West Virginia State Teachers' Association*. National Education Association, 1979.

Blanc, Eric. *Red State Revolt: The Teachers' Strikes and Working-Class Politics*. Verso, 2019.

Brecher, Jeremy. *Strike!* Straight Arrow Books, 1972.

Brenner, Aaron, Robert Brenner, and Cal Winslow, eds. *Rebel Rank and File: Labor Militancy and Revolt from Below During the Long 1970s*. Verso, 2010.

Burns, Joe. *Strike Back: Using the Militant Tactics of Labor's Past to Reignite Public Sector Unionism Today*. Ig Publishing, 2014.

Catte, Elizabeth, Emily Hilliard, and Jessica Salfia, eds. *55 Strong: Inside the West Virginia Teachers' Strike*. Belt Publishing, 2018.

Clark, Paul F. *The Miners' Fight for Democracy: Arnold Miller and the Reform of the United Mine Workers*. New York State School of Industrial and Labor Relations, 1981.

Cleaver, William. "Wildcats in the Appalachian Coal Fields." *Zerowork* 1 (December, 1975): 113–26. Reprinted in Midnight Notes Collective, eds. *Midnight Oil: Work, Energy, War, 1973–1992*. Autonomedia, 1992: 169–83.

Cohen, Sheila. *Ramparts of Resistance: Why Workers Lost Their Power and How to Get it Back*. Pluto Press, 2006.

Cooper, Laura J. "Discipline and Discharge of Public-Sector Employees: An Empirical Study of Arbitration Awards." *ABA Journal of Labor and Employment Law* 27, no. 2 (Winter 2012) 195–210.

Cooper, Melinda. "The Last Days of Sound Finance." *Phenomenal World*, July 26, 2022.

Corbin, David A. "Betrayal in the West Virginia Coal Fields: Eugene V. Debs and the Socialist Party of America, 1912–1914." *Journal of American History* 64, no. 4 (March, 1978): 987–1009.

Corbin, David Alan, ed. *Gun Thugs, Rednecks, and Radicals: A Documentary History of the West Virginia Mine Wars.* PM Press, 2011.

Corbin, David Alan. *Life, Work, and Rebellion in the Coal Fields: The Southern West Virginia Miners, 1880–1922.* University of Illinois Press, 1981.

Cormier, David, and David Michael. *Final Report of a Study of the West Virginia Public Sector Grievance Procedures.* Institute for Labor Studies and Research, West Virginia University, March 1, 2006.

Cornell, Herbert W. "Collective Bargaining by Public Employee Groups." *University of Pennsylvania Law Review* 107 (1958): 43–64.

Cudahy, Sarah W., William A. Herbert, and John F. Wirenius. "Total Eclipse of the Court: *Janus v. AFSCME, Council 31* in Historical, Legal, and Public Policy Contexts." *Hofstra Labor & Employment Law Journal* 36, no. 1 (Fall 2018): 55–122.

Dannin, Ellen. *Taking Back the Workers' Law: How to Fight the Assault on Labor Rights.* Cornell University Press, 2006.

Davidov, Guy. "Collective Bargaining Laws: Purpose and Scope." *International Journal of Comparative Labour Law and Industrial Relations* 81, no. 106 (2004): 1–20.

Derickson, Alan. "Down Solid: The Origins and Development of the Black Lung Insurgency." *Journal of Public Health Policy* 4, no. 1 (March 1983): 25–44.

Dilger, Robert Jay, Eleanor H. Blakely, Melissa Latimer, and Barry L. Locke. *Welfare Reform in West Virginia.* West Virginia University Press, 2004.

Dyke, Erin, and Brendan Muckian-Bates. "Educators Striking for a Better World: The Significance of Social Movement and Solidarity Unionisms." *Berkeley Review of Education* 9, no. 1 (2019).

Dyke, Erin, and Brendan Muckian-Bates. *Rank-and-File Rebels: Theories of Power and Change in the 2018 Education Strikes.* University Press of Colorado, 2023.

Edwards, Phil. *Status Report on Public Employee Organization in West Virginia.* Southern West Virginia Center for Labor Management Initiatives, 1992.

Fetherling, Dale. *Mother Jones: The Miners' Angel.* Southern Illinois University Press, 1974.

Feurer, Rosemary. *Radical Unionism in the Midwest, 1900–1950.* University of Illinois Press, 2006.

Fink, Leon, and Brian Greenberg. *Upheaval in the Quiet Zone: A History of Hospital Workers' Union, Local 1199.* University of Illinois Press, 1989.

Fitch, Robert. *Solidarity for Sale: How Corruption Destroyed the Labor Movement and Undermined America's Promise.* Public Affairs, 2006.

Fletcher, Bill Jr., and Fernando Gapasin. *Solidarity Divided: The Crisis in Organized Labor and a New Path Toward Social Justice.* University of California Press, 2008.

Foner, Philip D. *The Great Labor Uprising of 1877.* Monad Press, 1977.

Gentili, Dario. *The Age of Precarity: Endless Crisis as an Art of Government.* Verso, 2021.

Givan, Rebecca Kolins, and Amy Schrager Lang, eds. *Strike for the Common Good: Fighting for the Future of Public Education.* University of Michigan Press, 2020.

Gooding, Frederick W. Jr., and Eric S. Yellin, eds. *Public Workers in Service of America.* University of Illinois Press, 2023.

Gorby, William Hal. "'Balancing the Budget on the Back of Education': Neoliberalism and the 1990 West Virginia Teachers' Strike." *West Virginia History: A Journal of Regional Studies* 17 no. 1 (Spring 2023): 31–67.

Goulden, Joseph C. *Jerry Wurf: Labor's Last Angry Man.* Atheneum, 1982.

Green, James. *The Devil Is Here in These Hills: West Virginia's Coal Miners and Their Battle for Freedom.* Atlantic Monthly Press, 2015.

Gross, James A. *Broken Promises: The Subversion of U.S. Labor Relations Policy, 1947–1994.* Temple University Press, 1995.

Guerin, Daniel. *100 Years of Labor in the USA.* Ink Links, 1979.

Hanslowe, Kurt L. and John L. Acierno, "Law and Theory of Strikes by Government Employees." *Cornell Law Review* 67 (1982): 1055–83.

Harless, Rod. *The West Virginia Establishment.* Appalachian Movement Press, 1971.

Harris, Evelyn L.K., and Frank J. Krebs. *From Humble Beginnings: West Virginia State Federation of Labor.* West Virginia Labor History Publishing Fund, 1960.

Harvey, David. *A Brief History of Neoliberalism.* Oxford University Press, 2005.

Hassan, Abdullah Wais. *Unreliable Allies: Democrats and the Decline of Public Sector Unions.* University of California Santa Cruz, 2017.

Hennen, John. *A Union for Appalachian Healthcare Workers: The Radical Roots and Hard Fights of Local 1199.* West Virginia University Press, 2021.

Hennen, John. "Struggle for Recognition: The Marshall University Students for a Democratic Society and the Red Scare in Huntington, 1965–1969." *West Virginia History* 52 (1993): 127–47.

Hilliard, Emily. "The Daughters of Mother Jones: Lessons of Care Work and Labor Struggle in the Expressive Culture of the West Virginia Teachers' Strike." In *Making Our Future: Visionary Folklore and Everyday Culture in Appalachia.* University of North Carolina Press, 2022.

Hodges, Ann C., and William Warwick. "The Sheathed Sword: Public-Sector Union Efficacy in Non-Bargaining States." *ABA Journal of Labor and Employment Law* 27, no. 2 (Winter 2012): 275–92.

Honey, Michael K. *Going Down Jericho Road: The Memphis Strike, Martin Luther King's Last Campaign.* W.W. Norton and Sons, 2008.

Howard, Christopher. *The Welfare State Nobody Knows: Debunking Myths About U.S. Social Policy.* Princeton University Press, 2007.

Hower, Joseph E. "Jerry Wurf, the Rise of AFSCME, and the Fate of Labor Liberalism, 1947–1981." PhD diss., Georgetown University, 2013.

Kincaid, Charles M. "Resolving Public Employment Disputes: A Guide for West Virginia." *West Virginia Law Review* 79 (1976): 23–105.

Kreiser, Christine M. "A Rumbling Down Below: Miners for Democracy," *Goldenseal* (Fall 2018): 58–67.

Lofaso, Anne Marie. "In Defense of Public Sector Unions." *Hofstra Labor and Employment Law Journal* 28, no. 2 (2011): 301–34.

Lunt, Richard D. *Law and Order vs. the Miners: West Virginia, 1907–1933.* Appalachian Editions, 1992.

Lydersen, Kari. *Revolt on Goose Island: The Chicago Factory Takeover and What it Says about the Economic Crisis.* Melville House Publishing, 2009.

Lynd, Alice, and Staughton Lynd. *Rank and File: Personal Histories by Working-Class Organizers.* Beacon Press, 1973.

Lynd, Staughton. "John L. Lewis and His Critics: Some Forgotten Labor History That Still Matters Today." *Class, Race and Corporate Power* 5, no. 2 (2017).

Lynd, Staughton, and Daniel Gross. *Labor Law for the Rank and Filer: Building Solidarity While Staying Clear of the Law*. PM Press, 2008.

Malin, Martin H. "The Legislative Upheaval in Public-Sector Labor Law: A Search for Common Elements." *ABA Journal of Labor and Employment Law* 27, no. 2 (Winter 2012): 149–64.

Martin, Julian. *The Soviet Union and Lincoln County USA*. Published by the author, 2014.

Mau, Søren. *Mute Compulsion: A Marxist Theory of the Economic Power of Capital*. Verso, 2023.

McPherson, Michael Wayne. "Study of the Attitudes of Educational Leaders in West Virginia Toward Collective Bargaining and Selected Demographic Variables." PhD diss., Virginia Polytechnic Institute and State University, 1986.

Mooney, Fred. *Struggle in the Coal Fields: The Autobiography of Fred Mooney*. West Virginia University Library, 1967.

Morris, Charles J. *The Blue Eagle at Work: Reclaiming Democratic Rights in the American Workplace*. Cornell University Press, 2005.

Murolo, Priscilla. "Five Lessons from the History of Public Sector Unions." *Labor Notes*, June 11, 2018.

Murphy, Marjorie. *Blackboard Unions: The AFT and the NEA, 1900–1980*. Cornell University Press, 1990.

Ness, Immanuel, ed. *New Forms of Workers Organization: The Syndicalist and Autonomist Restoration of Class-Struggle Unionism*. PM Press, 2014.

Nyden, Linda, and Paul Nyden. "Showdown in Coal: The Struggle for Rank-and-File Unionism." Published by authors, 1978.

Nyden, Paul. "Miners for Democracy: Struggle in the Coal Fields." PhD diss., Department of Sociology, University of Pittsburgh, 1974.

Nyden, Paul. "Rank-and-File Organizations and the United Mine Workers of America." *Insurgent Sociologist* (Fall 1978): 25–39.

O'Connor, James. *Accumulation Crisis*. Basil Blackwell, 1984.

O'Connor, James. *The Fiscal Crisis of the State*. St. Martin's Press: 1973.

Perry, Huey. *"They'll Cut off Your Project": A Mingo County Chronicle*. West Virginia University Press, 2011.

Pope, Jim. "Labor's Constitution of Freedom." *Yale Law Review* 106, no. 94 (1997): 941–1031.

Pope, Jim. "The Western Pennsylvania Coal Strike of 1933, Part II: Lawmaking from Above and the Demise of Democracy in the United Mine Workers." *Labor History* 44, no. 2(2003): 259ff.

Pope, Jim. "Worker Lawmaking, Sit-Down Strikes, and the Shaping of American Industrial Relations, 1935–1958." *Law and History Review* 24, no. 1 (Spring, 2006): 45–113.

Report to the Governor of the Blue Ribbon Personnel Commission. December 1992.

Sartre, Jean-Paul. *Critique of Dialectical Reason: Volume 1, Theory of Practical Ensembles*. New Left Books, 1976.

Savage, Lon K. *Thunder in the Mountains: The West Virginia Mine War 1920–21*. Jalamap Publications, 1984.

Savage, Lon Kelly, and Ginny Savage Ayers. *Never Justice, Never Peace: Mother Jones and the Miner Rebellion at Paint and Cabin Creeks*. West Virginia University Press, 2018.

Secunda, Paul M. "The Wisconsin Public-Sector Labor Dispute of 2011." *ABA Journal of Labor and Employment Law* 27, no. 2 (Winter 2012) 293–306.

Shogan, Robert. *The Battle of Blair Mountain: The Story of America's Largest Labor Uprising*. Westview Press, 2004.

Slater, Joseph E. *Public Workers: Government Employees Unions, the Law, and the State, 1900–1962*. Cornell University Press, 2004.

Steel, Edward M., ed. *The Speeches and Writings of Mother Jones*. University of Pittsburgh Press, 1988.

Taft, Philip. *The A.F. of L. from the Death of Gompers to the Merger*. Octagon Books, 1970.

Tait, Vanessa. *Poor Workers' Unions: Rebuilding Labor from Below*. South End Press, 2005.

Van Deusen, David. *Insurgent Labor: The Vermont AFL-CIO, 2017–2023*. PM Press, 2024.

White, Ahmed A. "The Crime of Industrial Radicalism: Criminal Syndicalist Laws and the Industrial Workers of the World, 1917–1927." *Oregon Law Review* 85, no. 617 (2006), 649–69.

White, Ahmed A. *Under the Iron Heel: The Wobblies and the Capitalist War on Radical Workers*. University of California Press, 2022.

White, Ahmed A. "Workers Disarmed: The Campaign Against Mass Picketing and the Dilemma of Liberal Labor Rights." *Harvard Civil Rights-Civil Liberties Law Review* 49 (2014).

Winslow, Cal. *Labor's Civil War in California: The NUHW Healthcare Workers' Rebellion*. PM Press, 2010.

Young, James. *Union Power: The United Electrical Workers in Erie, Pennsylvania*. Monthly Review Press, 2017.

Ziegler, Robert H. *John L. Lewis: Labor Leader*. Twayne Publishers, 1988.

Index

"Passim" (literally "scattered") indicates intermittent discussion of a topic over a cluster of pages.

About the Author

Gordon Simmons is employed as an adjunct professor in philosophy at Marshall University and as a public defense investigator for the state of West Virginia. He is president of the West Virginia Labor History Association and, in addition to having served as the first chief steward of the West Virginia Public Workers Union, has been a member of the IWW, CWA Local 2001, AFSCME Local 3248, UE Local 170, and the state employee local of WVSSPA/UMWA.

ABOUT PM PRESS

PM Press is an independent, radical publisher of critically necessary books for our tumultuous times. Our aim is to deliver bold political ideas and vital stories to all walks of life and arm the dreamers to demand the impossible. Founded in 2007 by a small group of people with decades of publishing, media, and organizing experience, we have sold millions of copies of our books, most often one at a time, face to face. We're old enough to know what we're doing and young enough to know what's at stake. Join us to create a better world.

PM Press
PO Box 23912
Oakland, CA 94623
www.pmpress.org

PM Press in Europe
europe@pmpress.org
www.pmpress.org.uk

FRIENDS OF PM PRESS

These are indisputably momentous times—the financial system is melting down globally and the Empire is stumbling. Now more than ever there is a vital need for radical ideas.

In the many years since its founding—and on a mere shoestring—PM Press has risen to the formidable challenge of publishing and distributing knowledge and entertainment for the struggles ahead. With hundreds of releases to date, we have published an impressive and stimulating array of literature, art, music, politics, and culture. Using every available medium, we've succeeded in connecting those hungry for ideas and information to those putting them into practice.

Friends of PM allows you to directly help impact, amplify, and revitalize the discourse and actions of radical writers, filmmakers, and artists. It provides us with a stable foundation from which we can build upon our early successes and provides a much-needed subsidy for the materials that can't necessarily pay their own way. You can help make that happen—and receive every new title automatically delivered to your door once a month—by joining as a Friend of PM Press. And, we'll throw in a free T-shirt when you sign up.

Here are your options:

- **$30 a month** Get all books and pamphlets plus a 50% discount on all webstore purchases
- **$40 a month** Get all PM Press releases (including CDs and DVDs) plus a 50% discount on all webstore purchases
- **$100 a month** Superstar—Everything plus PM merchandise, free downloads, and a 50% discount on all webstore purchases

For those who can't afford $30 or more a month, we have **Sustainer Rates** at $15, $10 and $5. Sustainers get a free PM Press T-shirt and a 50% discount on all purchases from our website.

Your Visa or Mastercard will be billed once a month, until you tell us to stop. Or until our efforts succeed in bringing the revolution around. Or the financial meltdown of Capital makes plastic redundant. Whichever comes first.

Gun Thugs, Rednecks, and Radicals: A Documentary History of the West Virginia Mine Wars

Edited by David Alan Corbin

ISBN: 978-1-60486-452-6
$21.95 288 pages

Strikes and union battles occurred throughout American industry during the early part of the twentieth century, but none of these stories compare to the West Virginia Mine Wars of 1912 and 1921. These two workers' rebellions quickly drew national attention to an area known principally for its "black gold," the coal that was vital for U.S. factories, power plants, and warships of that age.

In 1912, miners struck against the harsh conditions in the work camps of Paint and Cabin Creeks and coal operators responded with force. The ensuing battles caused the West Virginia governor to declare martial law, prompting Samuel Gompers to dub the state "Russianized West Virginia [where] the people can be naught but serfs."

There was little improvement in working conditions by 1921, when another army—thousands of union miners—went up against similar numbers of state police, local deputies, and paid company guards. The weeklong Battle of Blair Mountain ended only after President Warren Harding sent 2,000 U.S. troops and a small unit of bombers to pacify the region

Gun Thugs, Rednecks, and Radicals tells the story of these union battles as seen by the leaders, rank-and-file participants, and the journalists who came to West Virginia to cover them for papers including *The Nation* and the *New York Times*.

Union leaders like Gompers, Frank Keeney, Fred Mooney, Bill Blizzard, and Mother Jones discuss the lives and struggles of the miners for their union. The book also contains articles, speeches, and personal testimony heard by two U.S. Senate committees sent to investigate West Virginia's labor problems. In this testimony, miners and their family members describe life and work in the coal camps, telling why they participated in these violent episodes in West Virginia history.

Special attention is given to the role of Huntington's own radical newspaper, *The Socialist and Labor Star*, a forgotten monument in the history of American heresy and radicalism.

Black Coal and Red Bandanas: An Illustrated History of the West Virginia Mine Wars

Raymond Tyler, illustrated by Summer McClinton and edited by Paul Buhle with an Introduction by Shaun Slifer and a Foreword by Gordon Simmons

ISBN: 979-8-88744-059-0
$19.95 136 pages

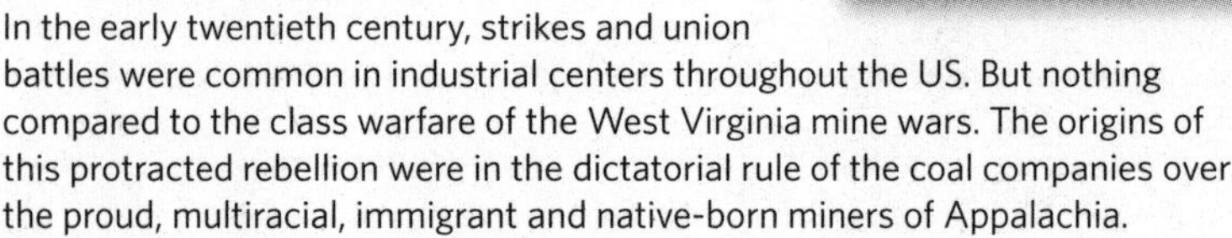

In the early twentieth century, strikes and union battles were common in industrial centers throughout the US. But nothing compared to the class warfare of the West Virginia mine wars. The origins of this protracted rebellion were in the dictatorial rule of the coal companies over the proud, multiracial, immigrant and native-born miners of Appalachia.

Our illustrated history begins with Mary Harris "Mother" Jones's arrival at the turn of the century. Whitehaired, matronly, and fiercely socialist, Jones became known as the "miners' angel" and helped turn the fledgling United Mine Workers into the nation's most powerful labor union. "Pray for the dead and fight like hell for the living" was her famous battle cry.

In 1912, miners led by stubborn Frank Keeney struck against harsh conditions in the work camps of Paint and Cabin Creeks. Coal operators responded by enlisting violent Baldwin-Felts guards. The ensuing battles and murderous events caused the governor to declare and execute martial law on a scale unprecedented in the US.

On May 19, 1920, in response to evictions by coal company agents, gunshots rang through the streets of a small town in "Bloody Mingo" county. In an event soon known as the "Matewan Massacre"; the pro-union, quick-draw chief of police Smilin' Sid Hatfield became an unexpected celebrity—but also a marked man.

Events climax with the dramatic Battle of Blair Mountain that pitched the spontaneous Red Neck Army of ten thousand armed strikers against a paid army of gun thugs in the largest labor uprising in US history and the largest armed uprising since the American Civil War.

This graphic interpretation of people's history features unforgettable main characters while also displaying the diverse rank and file workers who stood in solidarity during this struggle.

"It is past time to use the unique attributes of graphic arts to tell the remarkable story of the West Virginia Mine Wars. **Black Coal and Red Bandanas** *applies the stark colors of its title to allow the reader to visualize the world in which it is set."*
—Denise Giardina, author of *Storming Heaven*

Labor Power and Strategy

John Womack Jr.
Edited by Peter Olney and Glenn Perusek

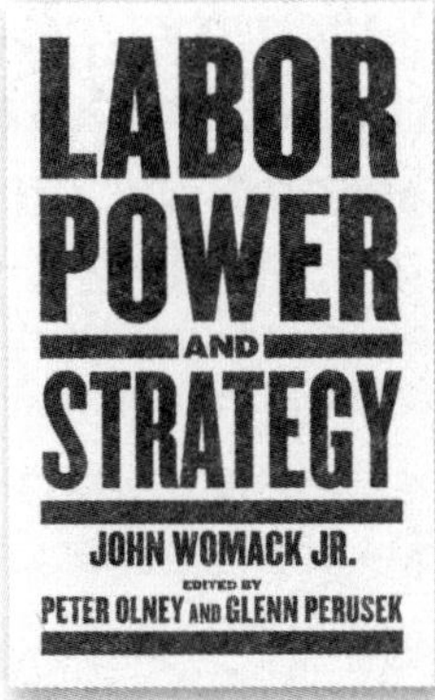

ISBN: 978-1-62963-974-1
$16.95 192 pages

What would it take to topple Amazon? To change how health care works in America? To break up the media monopolies that have taken hold of our information and imaginations? How is it possible to organize those without hope working on the margins? In *Labor Power and Strategy*, legendary strategist, historian and labor organizer John Womack speaks directly to a new generation, providing rational, radical, experience-based perspectives that help target and run smart, strategic, effective campaigns in the working class.

In this sleek, practical, pocket inspiration, Womack lays out a timely plan for identifying chokepoints and taking advantage of supply chain issues in order to seize and build labor power and solidarity. Interviewed by Peter Olney of the International Longshore and Warehouse Union, Womack's lively, illuminating thoughts are built upon by ten young labor organizers and educators, whose responses create a rich dialogue and open a space for joyful, achievable change. With stories of triumph that will bring readers to tears this back-pocket primer is an instant classic.

"In Our Revolution we shout, 'When we Organize, We Win,' but organize who and win what? Labor Power and Strategy *is a great collection of Womack and 10 organizers debating strategic workplace organizing vs associational or more general organizing at workplaces or in communities. Womack, in a long initial interview and in the conclusion, argues that without organizing workplace chokepoints, we are left with the spontaneous movements that come and go. Several of the 10 organizers essentially argue that the spontaneous can become conscious and long lasting. Grab the book and take up the debate."*
—Larry Cohen, board chair of Our Revolution, past president of Communications Workers of America

"In this fascinating and insightful dialogue, the distinguished historian John Womack and a set of veteran labor activists probe the most fundamental of questions: How do we organize the 21 century working class and give it the power to transform world capitalism? Are workers with vital skills and strategic leverage the key to a labor resurgence, or should organizers wager upon a mobilization of working people whose relationship to the economy's commanding heights is more diffuse? Or can we arrive at some dialectical symbiosis? Whatever the answer, this is the kind of constructively radical conversation essential to the rebirth of working-class power in our time."
—Nelson Lichtenstein, historian and author of *Capitalism Contested: The New Deal and Its Legacies*

Solidarity Unionism: Rebuilding the Labor Movement from Below, Second Edition

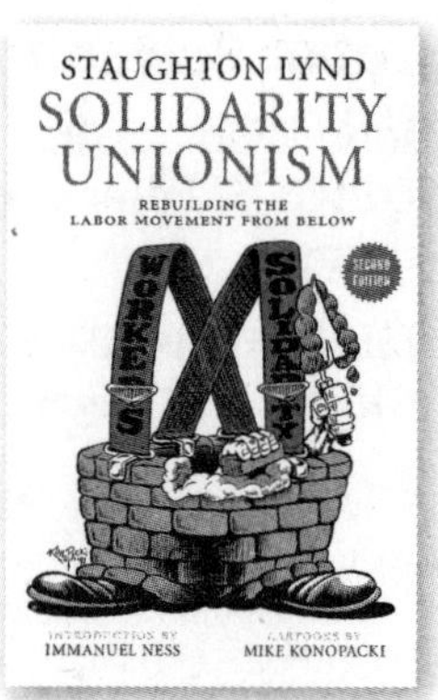

Staughton Lynd with an Introduction by Immanuel Ness and iIllustrations by Mike Konopacki

ISBN: 978-1-62963-096-0
$14.95 128 pages

Solidarity Unionism is critical reading for all who care about the future of labor. Drawing deeply on Staughton Lynd's experiences as a labor lawyer and activist in Youngstown, OH, and on his profound understanding of the history of the Congress of Industrial Organizations (CIO), *Solidarity Unionism* helps us begin to put not only movement but also vision back into the labor movement.

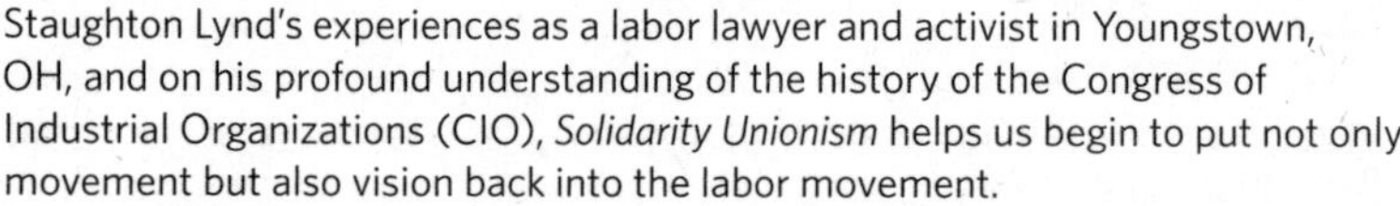

While many lament the decline of traditional unions, Lynd takes succor in the blossoming of rank-and-file worker organizations throughout the world that are countering rapacious capitalists and those comfortable labor leaders that think they know more about work and struggle than their own members. If we apply a new measure of workers' power that is deeply rooted in gatherings of workers and communities, the bleak and static perspective about the sorry state of labor today becomes bright and dynamic.

To secure the gains of solidarity unions, Lynd has proposed parallel bodies of workers who share the principles of rank-and-file solidarity and can coordinate the activities of local workers' assemblies. Detailed and inspiring examples include experiments in workers' self-organization across industries in steel-producing Youngstown, as well as horizontal networks of solidarity formed in a variety of US cities and successful direct actions overseas.

This is a tradition that workers understand but labor leaders reject. After so many failures, it is time to frankly recognize that the century-old system of recognition of a single union as exclusive collective bargaining agent was fatally flawed from the beginning and doesn't work for most workers. If we are to live with dignity, we must collectively resist. This book is not a prescription but reveals the lived experience of working people continuously taking risks for the common good.

"Solidarity Unionism *is an essential text for all rank-and-file workers as well as labor activists. Beautifully succinct, it outlines how CIO unions grew into an ineffectual model for rank-and-file empowerment, and provides examples of how alternative labor organizations have flourished in the wake of this. Lynd illustrates to a new generation of workers that we do have alternatives, and his call for a qualitatively different kind of labor organization gives us an ideological and strategic framework that we can apply in our day-to-day struggles on the shop floor."*
—Diane Krauthamer, *Industrial Worker*

Strike! 50th Anniversary Edition

Jeremy Brecher with a Preface by Sara Nelson and a Foreword by Kim Kelly

ISBN: 978-1-62963-800-3 (paperback)
978-1-62963-856-0 (hardcover)
$28.95/$60.00 640 pages

Jeremy Brecher's *Strike!* narrates the dramatic story of repeated, massive, and sometimes violent revolts by ordinary working people in America. Involving nationwide general strikes, the seizure of vast industrial establishments, nonviolent direct action on a massive scale, and armed battles with artillery and tanks, this exciting hidden history is told from the point of view of the rank-and-file workers who lived it. Encompassing the repeated repression of workers' rebellions by company-sponsored violence, local police, state militias, and the US Army and National Guard, it reveals a dimension of American history rarely found in the usual high school or college history course.

Since its original publication in 1972, no book has done as much as *Strike!* to bring US labor history to a wide audience. Now this fiftieth anniversary edition brings the story up to date with chapters covering the "mini-revolts of the 21st century," including Occupy Wall Street and the Fight for Fifteen. The new edition contains over a hundred pages of new materials and concludes by examining a wide range of current struggles, ranging from #BlackLivesMatter, to the great wave of teachers strikes "for the soul of public education," to the global "Student Strike for Climate," that may be harbingers of mass strikes to come.

"Jeremy Brecher's Strike! *is a classic of American historical writing. This new edition, bringing his account up to the present, comes amid rampant inequality and growing popular resistance. No book could be more timely for those seeking the roots of our current condition."*
—Eric Foner, Pulitzer Prize winner and DeWitt Clinton Professor of History at Columbia University

"Magnificent—a vivid, muscular labor history, just updated and rereleased by PM Press, which should be at the side of anyone who wants to understand the deep structure of force and counterforce in America."
—JoAnn Wypijewski, author of *Killing Trayvons: An Anthology of American Violence*

"An exciting history of American labor. Brings to life the flashpoints of labor history. Scholarly, genuinely stirring."
—*New York Times*

Y'all Means All: The Emerging Voices Queering Appalachia

Edited by Z. Zane McNeill

ISBN: 978-1-62963-914-7
$20.00 200 pages

Y'all Means All is a celebration of the weird and wonderful aspects of a troubled region in all of their manifest glory! This collection is a thought-provoking hoot and a holler of "we're queer and we're here to stay, cause we're every bit a piece of the landscape as the rocks and the trees" echoing through the hills of Appalachia and into the boardrooms of every media outlet and opportunistic author seeking to define Appalachia from the outside for their own political agendas. Multidisciplinary and multigenre, *Y'all* necessarily incorporates elements of critical theory, such as critical race theory and queer theory, while dealing with a multitude of methodologies, from quantitative analysis, to oral history and autoethnography.

This collection eschews the contemporary trend of "reactive" or "responsive" writing in the genre of Appalachian studies, and alternatively, provides examples of how modern Appalachians are defining themselves on their own terms. As such, it also serves as a toolkit for other Appalachian readers to follow suit, and similarly challenge the labels, stereotypes, and definitions often thrust upon them. While providing blunt commentary on the region's past and present, the book's soul is sustained by the resilience, ingenuity, and spirit exhibited by the authors, values which have historically characterized the Appalachian region and are continuing to define its culture to the present.

This book demonstrates above all else that Appalachia and its people are filled with a vitality and passion for their region which will slowly but surely effect long-lasting and positive changes in the region. If historically Appalachia has been treated as a "mirror" of the country, this book breaks that trend by allowing modern Appalachians to examine their own reflections and to share their insights in an honest, unfiltered manner with the world.

"These deeply personal and theoretically informed essays explore the fight for social justice and inclusivity in Appalachia through the intersections of environmental action, LGBTQA+ representational politics, antiracism, and movements for disability justice. This Appalachia is inhabited by a queer temporality and geography, where gardening lore teaches us that seeds dance into plants in their own time, not according to a straight-edged neoliberal discipline."

—Rebecca Scott, author of *Removing Mountains: Extracting Nature and Identity in the Appalachian Coalfields*